# CAMBRIDGE STUDIES IN LINGUISTICS

*General Editors* · W. SIDNEY ALLEN · B. COMRIE · C. J. FILLMORE
E. J. A. HENDERSON · F. W. HOUSEHOLDER · R. LASS · J. LYONS
R. B. LE PAGE · F. R. PALMER · R. POSNER · J. L. M. TRIM

*Studies in the acquisition of deictic terms*

# In this series

# STUDIES IN THE ACQUISITION OF DEICTIC TERMS

## CHRISTINE TANZ

*Assistant Professor of Psychology, University of Arizona*

CAMBRIDGE UNIVERSITY PRESS

CAMBRIDGE

LONDON   NEW YORK   NEW ROCHELLE

MELBOURNE   SYDNEY

CAMBRIDGE UNIVERSITY PRESS
Cambridge, New York, Melbourne, Madrid, Cape Town, Singapore, São Paulo, Delhi

Cambridge University Press
The Edinburgh Building, Cambridge CB2 8RU, UK

Published in the United States of America by Cambridge University Press, New York

www.cambridge.org
Information on this title: www.cambridge.org/9780521103237

First published 1980
This digitally printed version 2009

*A catalogue record for this publication is available from the British Library*

*Library of Congress Cataloguing in Publication data*

Tanz, Christine.
Studies in the acquisition of deictic terms.

(Cambridge Studies in linguistics; 26)
Includes index.
1. Language acquisition. 2. Grammar, Comparative
and general—Deixis. I. Title. II. Series.
P118.T34   415   79-12272

ISBN 978-0-521-22740-7 hardback
ISBN 978-0-521-10323-7 paperback

# Contents

# List of illustrations and tables

# Acknowledgments

I would like to thank Wilbur Hass, my first psycholinguistics professor, for telling me the name of the phenomenon I was interested in, and Charles Osgood for providing a congenial situation to pursue the interest and for continuing moral support. I am grateful to Tom Roeper, Bill Brewer, Janellen Huttenlocher, Lance Rips, Eve Clark, and Jill de Villiers for helpful discussions and comments at various stages of the enterprise. I benefited enormously from the careful reading and detailed comments of Charles Fillmore and Lise Menn. And I especially thank my advisor, David McNeill, for his advice and patient encouragement.

The project that was begun at the University of Chicago and carried out at the University of Illinois underwent its final revisions at the University of Arizona. Having thanked my friends and teachers at the former institutions, I would also like to acknowledge the support of my friends and colleagues at the current one: Susan Philips, Adrian Akmajian, Keith and Adrienne Lehrer, Ken and Yetta Goodman, Lon Wheeler, Neil Bartlett.

The encouragement of several other people was immeasurably helpful to me across the time in Chicago, Champaign, and Tucson. I would like to express my gratitude to them: Henry and Renee Tanz, Jane Stevens, and Fritz Larsen.

# 1 *The acquisition of deictic terms*

## Deixis

When language is spoken, it occurs in a specific location, at a specific time, is produced by a specific person and is (usually) addressed to some specific other person or persons. Only written language can ever be free of this kind of anchoring in the extra-linguistic situation. A sentence on a slip of paper can move through space and time, 'speaker'-less, and addressee-less. All natural, spoken languages have devices that link the utterance with its spatio-temporal and personal context. This linkage is called 'deixis.' Personal pronouns are paradigmatic deictic terms. Verb tense is a deictic device. Other deictic terms and terms incorporating deictic elements will be discussed later.

In his classification of signs into symbols, indices, and icons, Peirce placed deictic terms in a category intermediate between symbols and indices (Burks, 1949). Peirce's classification is based on the idea that there are different ways in which one thing can 'signify' another. Let us take the example of a house. One way to signify 'house' is by using the word *house*. The word is associated with the object by conventional rule. This classifies it as a *symbol*. As Burks points out, all words are symbols because they are associated with their objects by conventional rules. A blueprint of a house also serves as a sign of a house. It does so by exhibiting the same structure. This classifies it as an *icon*. Finally, one can also 'signify' a house by the act of pointing at it. Pointing calls attention to the house directly or, in Peirce's terminology, by standing in an 'existential relation' to it. Pointing is the prototype of an *index*. According to Burks, a symbol can be said to denote a house, an icon to exhibit or exemplify it, and an index to indicate it.

Deictic terms partake of two sign functions. For example, the pronoun *I* is a symbol insofar as it is a conventionalized term, arbitrarily different from *you*, and from its equivalent in other languages. It is an index in that it refers to the person uttering it. It 'cannot represent its object without being in existential relation [to it]' (Jakobson, 1957). Because of this combination of functions, Peirce classifies deictic terms as 'indexical symbols.'

Jakobson focuses on the *combination* of functions in making the claim that deictic terms, or 'shifters' as he calls them, are 'a complex category ... [that belong] to the late acquisitions of child language and to the early losses of aphasia ... It is quite obvious,' Jakobson goes on, 'that the child who has learned to identify himself with his proper name will not easily become accustomed to such alienable terms as the personal pronouns.'

Lyons (1975), on the other hand, focuses exclusively on the indexical function of deictic particles in his argument that they are primitive and ontogenetically prior to other referring expressions. The claims of Jakobson and of Lyons are not incompatible. Lyons does not predict that correct use of *I/you/he* will be achieved early, or that *this* and *that* will be understood early in their contrastive sense. This level of knowledge depends precisely on the combining of the indexical function of these terms with their symbolic function. *I* is indexical, but specifically it is an index of the speaker. *You* is indexical, but specifically it is an index of the hearer. *This* and *that* are indexical, but they are specifically indexical of entities and, in their contrastive sense, of entities relatively near the speaker and relatively farther from the speaker.

What Lyons postulates to be primitive is a pure deictic particle, 'neutral with respect to any distinctions of gender or proximity' (p. 95), and presumably neutral with respect to participant roles in the speech act. The particle serving this function will be realized differently by different children. In English it seems often to derive from the demonstratives *this* and *that* and take forms like /di/, /dʌ/, etc. It reflects the focus of the child's attention and serves to direct another person's attention. Its general meaning, according to Lyons, is simply 'look!' or 'there!' And it is often accompanied by a gesture of the eyes, head, or hands, towards the entity or event in question. This description of terms serving a pure deictic function converges with a semantic category uniformly described by empirical researchers as being among the first to appear in children's speech. Brown (1973) and Bloom (1973) both distinguish between two major categories of early combinatorial utterances. One includes relational constructions such as agent–action whose overall meanings emerge out of abstract relations between the words.

The other is a small category that Brown calls 'operations of reference' in which he includes 'nomination,' 'recurrence,' and 'non-existence.' Bloom proposes similar categories, only substituting the term 'existence' for 'nomination.' Typical examples of the three would be 'that kitty,' 'more kitty,' and 'no kitty.' In these types of utterances, meaning is tied more to the lexical meaning of 'that,' 'more,' and 'no.' The words that most commonly serve the function of nomination or existence are the deictic demonstratives and locatives of adult language with or without referential labels attached to them and the definite and indefinite articles.

Brown reports that there are two prototypic situations in which nomination occurs. One is initiated by an adult asking 'What's that?' or 'Where's X?' In either case the adult knows the answer. Such questions give children the opportunity to indicate that they know the name of the object, in the first case (a production task) directly, by supplying the name, in the second (a comprehension task) indirectly, by supplying the correct location. The adult who initiates this language game is usually interested in the child's ability to label and recognize labels. But the game incidentally accomplishes another important effect, namely practice in the joint focusing of attention.

The second prototypic situation in which nomination occurs is one that the child initiates. The child typically says 'see' or 'this' or 'that' or 'there' about some object, sometimes also appending a name. Bloom glosses this type of usage as a comment on the 'existence' of a referent. Brown stresses its labeling function, the 'linking' of names and referents. The deictic interpretation is not completely distinct from these but has a different emphasis: the function of registering notice and directing notice to an object. Both intentions, labeling and noticing, can probably be attributed to children on different occasions.

Of the three basic operations of reference, nomination can be judged to be the most primitive by the fact that among the children surveyed by Brown almost every child who has any basic operation of reference has this one. A child who expresses the operations of 'recurrence' or 'non-existence' is highly likely also to express the operation of 'nomination.' The conditional probabilities in the opposite direction are not as high. The words that most commonly serve the operation of nomination are the words that are the deictic demonstratives and locatives of adult language plus the definite and indefinite articles.

Some of the indexical terms of nomination (*this, that, there*) first occur alone in early speech and then gradually with 'referential' terms But in early speech the distinction between deixis and full symbolic reference is in effect neutralized. Many observers have reported that at first children talk only about the contemporaneous situation. Under these circumstances nouns are used, as demonstratives or deictic personal pronouns must be, only in the presence of the objects to which they refer. This can be considered a kind of elaborated de facto deixis. McNeill (1975) develops the same point in 'Semiotic extension' and incorporates it into a theory of how children make the transition from the achievements of the sensory-motor level of intelligence to the beginnings of language. The nominational utterances should be considered *elaborated* deixis because *different* terms are used to point to different objects. Therefore the rudiments of the symbolic function are present. But the indexical function is uniformly present as well. We cannot confidently say that the distinction between deixis and fully fledged reference is operative until the child exploits the potential of nominal referential expressions by using them in the absence of their referents.

The principle of developmental economy formulated by Werner & Kaplan (1963) and extended by Slobin (1973) applies at this early juncture of language development. Werner & Kaplan made the generalization that new functions are first served by old forms. Slobin added a reciprocal generalization: new forms first express old functions. Here this principle is seen to apply at the onset of language, in the very leap into language itself. Common names, which bear the possibility of reference latent within them, are first used in the familiar and pre-verbal function of pointing. This emphasis on the pointing function of early speech is not meant to contradict the view that one-word utterances are holophrastic. They may also carry out a predicative function. But that is a separate issue. All that is claimed here is that first utterances involve an indexical component, whether or not they are also interpreted as being predications about the object of reference.

## Deixis and word realism

In the light of the preceding analysis of children's early utterances as *all* being indexical, we can take a new look at the phenomenon of word realism as described by Piaget. 'Word realism' describes children's tendency to treat names as inherent properties of objects. When questioned, children reveal a belief that if the name is changed, the object is also changed, and that the name is held by virtue of the object's possessing various other of its properties.

Could the sun have been called 'moon' and the moon 'sun'?
– *No.*
– Why not?
– *Because the sun shines brighter than the moon.*          (Piaget, 1967b: 81)

Stated in a different way, children who display word realism speak as if referential words were icons and indices rather than symbols. Although word realism is a meta-linguistic orientation that is incorrect from our point of view, it could be regarded as having a certain amount of validity – as a description of children's own initial language performance. In children's early output, names are indexical. They do not occur without their referents, and hence behave *like* attributes of the referents. Although to a much lesser degree, the same thing is true of referential terms in speech input to young children. If small children live, or at least speak, in 'the here and now,' adults will incline to join them there. But adults of course are also free to wander into the there and then.

It is possible to imagine that children arrive at word realism by the application of the same capacity for synthesis that enables them gradually to recognize various manifestations of an object as being the same object. By this account, word realism is an overgeneralization of object constancy.

The disparate manifestations of an object that are assimilated in the concept of that object comprise auditory and tactile impressions as well as various visual ones. On any single occasion of experiencing the object, not all of these manifestations are experienced simultaneously. This is the crux of the problem of object constancy. Children must *synthesize* the various perceptual manifestations into an integrated conceptual unit.

A name is yet one more (auditory) manifestation whose occurrence correlates strongly with other manifestations of an object. Along with everything else, the name is incorporated in the synthesis too. Although children do not *always* hear the name whenever the object is present, neither do they see each of its visual projections whenever they encounter the object. The final synthesis, when it is appropriate as well as when it is erroneous, is their own contribution, and does not depend on perfect correlation.

Before children produce language themselves they have no direct control over the apparent manifestation of an object that is that object's name. Unable to manipulate it, they have no opportunity to discover that it is detachable from its referent. When children do begin to speak, and thus to operate on names, they tend to use them in the presence of their referents and so the names remain, in effect, still attached to the referents. Only after children begin to use referential terms in their full symbolic capacity, i.e. in the absence of their referents, is the way paved for them to abandon word realism. But the meta-linguistic reorientation lags behind their behavioral achievement.

Fully fledged reference can be thought of as the liberation of the name from the requirement that its referent be present. We can regard the process of arriving at full referential expression as analogous to the process of interiorization, described by Piaget, through which children arrive at mental representations. In the latter case the image of an object becomes separate from the object; in the former, the name of the object becomes separate from the object.

## The symbolic component of indexical symbols

A pure index, such as the gesture of pointing, can be used to point to anything – a person, a location, an object. The deictic terms are not pure indices. As was discussed above, they are indexical *symbols*. Their meanings are not totally contextual. It is at the symbolic level that their general meanings are defined. Thus the personal pronouns are indices of persons. In particular *I* indexes the person uttering it, *you* the person addressed. These roles in the speech act are distinguished in all languages. *Here* and *there* are indices of location. *This* and *that* are indices of entities. Both pairs of terms involve a contrast along a dimension that is defined with respect to a deictic variable: proximity to the speaker. *In back of, in front of*, and *at the side of* are an interesting set of terms in that they can be used in a purely symbolic sense, or in an indexical sense. They express a spatial relationship with respect to some point of reference. In their symbolic sense the relationship is defined in terms of attributes inherent to the reference object, its permanent directional features. In the indexical sense of these expressions the spatial relationship is defined jointly by the position of the reference object and by the position of a participant in the speech act.

The motion verbs *come, go, bring,* and *take,* as Fillmore (1966, 1971e) has demonstrated, also involve deictic components in their meaning. To give a brief illustration, the question 'Are you coming to the beach?' presupposes something about the position of the speaker at the time of the utterance or at the time referred to in the utterance. The speaker must be at the location, the beach, at one of those two times in order for the sentence to be appropriate, or, at least, he must expect to be there. In other words, these verbs involve components of person deixis, place deixis, and time deixis as well. The semantics of these various deictic terms will be discussed in more detail in later chapters.

The problem of learning the correct use of the deictic terms does not turn on the indexical function per se but rather involves discovering the symbolic distinctions that are mapped by the deictic terms. However, the indexical properties of the deictic terms account for the special difficulty of discovering these distinctions, a type of difficulty not met with in purely symbolic terms. This will be discussed in the next section.

## Deixis and egocentrism

To use the deictic terms correctly, children must incorporate perspective as a component of meaning. They are addressed by name and as *you*, but must learn that while the name is a label for them, the *you* is not. The people who speak to children refer to themselves as *mommy* or *daddy*, etc., or as *I*. Children can address them as *mommy* or *daddy*, but not as *I*. To use the deictic terms correctly, with themselves at center, children must have grasped how other people use them, all with themselves at center. The ability to do this would seem to correspond exactly with an ability young children have been shown to lack. According to the analysis that children are cognitively egocentric, they cannot adopt points of view other than their own. De Villiers & de Villiers (1974) have also observed the relevance of children's mastery of deictic terms to an understanding of the boundaries of egocentrism.

It was in the sphere of language that Piaget first identified the phenomenon of cognitive egocentrism. Studying children's speech he observed patterns of repetition, of monologue, and of collective monologue that did not appear to serve a communicative function. He characterized noncommunicative speech as egocentric speech. The concept of egocentrism was subsequently extended by Piaget and other researchers to describe many aspects of children's cognitive orientation and behavior: moral judgment, reasoning, communication. Attempts have been made, with inconsistent results, to determine whether a single egocentrism factor underlies the various behavioral manifestations that have been attributed to egocentrism.

Recently a revisionary tide has begun, with a number of researchers demonstrating that children do attend to the speech of their interlocutors, and respond appropriately, both in terms of content and construction of messages (Garvey & Hogan, 1973; Maratsos, 1973; Keenan, 1974). Their evidence for nonegocentrism comes from research on topics identical to those in which the concept of egocentrism was defined and refined. The evidence that can be brought to bear from children's knowledge of deictic terms is a new kind of evidence, not discussed in the original formulations of egocentrism.

The full spectrum of egocentric phenomena ranges from children's inability to take someone else's perspective in the concrete, spatial sense to their inability to adopt a different perspective in the figurative sense. The classic example of the former is Piaget's three-mountain demonstration. Piaget showed children a three-dimensional model of a landscape with three mountains, a tree and a house. He then asked them to select a picture which represented what they saw in looking at the mountains. Later, he asked them to select pictures representing what a doll standing at some other location would see. Subjects showed different degrees of success in making an appropriate choice. The most illuminating failure was for children consistently to select the picture representing their own view. An example of failure to adopt another person's perspective in the figurative sense is the inability to guess what they might like as a present, as when a small boy, in an experimental task, selects a toy truck from a number of items as a good gift for his mother (Flavell, Botkin, Fry, Wright & Jarvis, 1968).

Flavell assumes that nonegocentrism, or role-taking, or to coin a term, 'perspectivism,' emerges first in the concrete sphere of visual perspective relative to objects in the environment. Subsequently it extends to perspective in the figurative sense. The language phenomenon, deixis, does not fall conveniently into either category. It lacks the component of an external physical situation which is constant despite changes of orientation and which permits changes of orientation to be reversed. On the other hand, it does not depend on making inferential judgments about the inner state of another person. An understanding of children's mastery of language that is inherently nonegocentric should contribute to our general knowledge of children's emergence from a state of relative egocentrism.

## Deixis and semantic theory

In the type of semantic theory which focuses on meaning as it resides in words and sentences, deictic terms are a marginal category, of no special theoretical interest. A different type of semantic theory attempts to represent how meaning resides in the integration of utterances with context (broadly defined). In such a theory the deictic terms suddenly become central. Rommetveit (1968) is one proponent of the view that the unit of communication is not the sentence, but the 'message' comprising 'two separate but mutually dependent components, namely the act of speech itself and a nonlinguistic component of the situation.' Feldman (1971) made the same point in arguing that most sentences are 'underdetermined' in that their meaning cannot be fully explicated on sentence-internal grounds, 'without reference to their existence in some speaker–hearer context.' She criticized linguists for dealing exclusively with fully determined sentences. In doing so she stopped short of the more radical claim that no sentences are fully determined. It is through the work of Grice (1967, 1971) and its interpretation by Gordon & Lakoff (1971) that this approach to semantics has come to be widely known and to influence some branches of linguistics and psycholinguistics. Grice's approach is encapsulated in the statement that sentences don't have meanings, only utterers do. Grice's tacit emphasis is on production; Rommetveit's on comprehension. But both stress that meaning does not reside in the sentence itself. And, as Rommetveit says, 'the most immediately transparent articulation between the act of speech and its behavioral setting is found in conjunction with components of linguistic media which are called "deictic signs."' In one sense of 'meaning,' the sense advanced by speech act theorists, the meaning of the now-famous sentence 'It's hot in here' depends on the context in which it is uttered, including the identity of the addressee and his relation to the speaker. In a similar sense, the meaning of *you* also depends on the context in which it is uttered. This is not merely a standard phenomenon of reference. Different acts of uttering *chair* may single out different chairs, just as different acts of uttering *you* single out different individuals, but the utterance does not establish the chair as a chair while it does establish an individual as the addressee.

It is the deictic terms that most clearly demonstrate that the principle of extra-linguistic contextual determination of meaning extends from the level of sentences to the lexical level.

These broad issues constitute the background for the series of investigations on the acquisition of deictic terms reported in the following chapters. The experiments test children's comprehension of the (singular) personal pronouns, the deictic use of *in front of* and *in back of*, the contrastive use of the demonstratives *this* and *that* and the locatives *here* and *there*, and their knowledge of the conditions for using *come* vs. *go* and *bring* vs. *take*. As far as possible, given that some children left school during the period of study, the same children were used as subjects in each experiment in order to permit intra-subject analyses. This allows us to see if there are invariant sequences of acquisition across individuals, in other words to determine if knowledge of one class of deictic terms is conditional upon knowledge of another.

A number of other topics are also taken up. Within sets of deictic terms, the order of acquisition is used to evaluate various current proposals about semantic development. Several hypotheses are discussed in detail, notably those of H. Clark and E. Clark: the hypotheses that unmarked terms are learned before marked terms, that conceptually positive terms are learned before conceptually negative ones, and, in general, that cognitive complexity is directly mirrored in semantic complexity which in turn is directly reflected in order of acquisition. Rather than elaborate these topics further here, I will discuss them in detail in the context of the actual experiments.

# 2 *Deictic and nondeictic spatial relations*

## The meaning of *in front of* and *in back of*

As everyone will agree who has ever tried to give or to follow directions for locating one object with respect to another, the meaning of the spatial prepositions *in front of* and *in back of* contains some ambiguities. Teller (1969) has illustrated the problem clearly with the example of a photographer asking his son to stand in front of a car in order to have his picture taken. The photographer himself is set up at some distance from the side of the car. The child could interpret the directions in two ways: either to stand at the headlight end of the car, or to stand at the side which the photographer is facing. In the first case he would be interpreting *in front of* in terms of the intrinsic front of the reference object. In the second case he would be treating *in front of* as a deictic expression, defined in terms of spatial relations between the reference object and the speaker.

Some objects, like the car in the example, have an 'intrinsic' front and back and sides. Others, like a tree, do not. The principles according to which intrinsic fronts and backs are defined are quite variable despite an essential unity which Teller tries to capture by identifying *front* with the feature (+prominent). Fillmore (1971b) has enumerated some of the criteria as follows: for an animal, the front is that section or side which has the main organs of perception and 'which arrives first whenever it moves in its most characteristic manner of movement' (p. 5). If a nonliving object in any way resembles an animal with a front and back, 'the portion of the object designated as its front is so designated on analogy with the associated model.' If the object has a characteristic orientation in motion, then again the part arriving first is the front. Fillmore's statement of the first-arrival criterion is a nice way of getting around the use of 'frontward' or 'forward' motion in defining 'front.'

These criteria are of course not always applicable. The front of a type-writer, for example, might be defined as the side toward which a user is normally oriented, and the front of a house that toward which users typically have access. There are numerous further complications. Fill-more points out that the front of a church by the access criterion is opposite the front by the user criterion; the front on the outside is opposite the front on the inside. And Teller tackles the problem of deciding which end is the front end of a telescope.

Were these criteria fully elaborated and broad enough to cover any contingency, one question would still remain: to what extent do people use them in recognizing the front or back of anything? It is possible that in real life they use instead a collection of scattered heuristics, which while correlated with the criteria set out above, may not have as broad or inclusive a formulation. For example, a person may recognize the front end of a car not by the general principle, also applicable to dogs, bicycles, worms, etc., that it is the first part to arrive, but by the fact that it is the end with the headlights. Headlights and first-arrival correlate strongly in cars but are not identical criteria.

Perhaps a distinction should be made between the maximally inclusive criteria linguists try to arrive at when they *define* the words *front* and *back*, and the criteria that speakers use when they *identify* the fronts and backs of objects. This is a restatement of the question of the psychological reality of a syntactic or semantic formulation. The degree to which children's identificational criteria approximate the linguists' definitional criteria will probably increase with development although they need never correspond exactly.

The minimum condition for an intrinsic front and back is some clear differentiation of sides. Objects that are radially symmetrical around a vertical axis do not have a front or back except as situationally defined. The 'front of the tree' takes on meaning only with respect to the position of the speaker or some other observer.

The spatial locations expressed in the prepositions *in front of* and *in back of* can have different meanings depending on whether the point of reference has an intrinsic front and back. If it does, then *in front of* can have an absolute sense: 'in the space near the front extremity.' Or it can have a deictic sense: usually 'in the space near the side closest to the speaker or some other observer.' If the reference object does not have an intrinsic front and back, then *in front of* it and *in back of* it are restricted to the deictic sense.

The duality of absolute vs. deictic meaning doesn't extend to the word *front* when it is used as a noun. The 'front of the car' is only the headlight end. Even if there is agreement that someone standing next to the door is standing in front of the car, that side can't be referred to as 'the front'. The deictic–absolute duality applies only to the phrasal derivatives of *front* and *back*: *in front of* and *in back of*.

Locative expressions work by specifying the position of the object in question with respect to some other reference object. In their deictic sense, *in front of* and *in back of*, are 'second order' locatives. They describe the position of an object with respect to a reference object with respect to a third object which is usually (but not always) a person. In 'the dog is in back of the hydrant,' the dog's position is expressed in relation to the position of the hydrant; but the orientation of the hydrant is defined, although not overtly described, in relation to the speaker or some other observer.

An unintroduced personage persists in creeping into this discussion: 'some other observer.' Neither the position of speaker nor of addressee is enough to specify fully the deictic sense of *in front of* and *in back of*. For example, neither one of them has to be at the source of the bullets in order to say: 'Bullets were flying, and the sheriff ducked behind a tree.' 'Behind a tree' here is defined by the direction of the bullets. The speaker and addressee could even be surveying the scene from a vantage point on the sheriff's side of the tree. If the gunfight ended, the sheriff's position vis-à-vis them would then be 'in front of a tree.' The 'other observer' is introduced to capture other sources of directionality besides the positions of the speaker and hearer. This deictic openness is one property that distinguishes *in front of* and *in back of* from *this* and *that*, and *here* and *there*, which are defined more strictly in terms of the location of speaker and hearer.

No other deictic system intersects with a nondeictic system of spatial expressions in the manner of *in front of/in back of* and *at the side of*. So this particular domain provides a unique opportunity to compare acquisition processes, and to determine the degree to which knowledge of the two systems is related.

Deictic terms viewed as egocentric terms

Previous research into the relation of deictic and nondeictic *front/back/side* has approached the subject from a different perspective from the one outlined above although experiments have had a similar structure to those discussed here. Harris & Strommen (1972a) imply that the deictic system of spatial relations is 'egocentric' because it incorporates the speaker's perspective. They interpret the contrast between the absolute and the deictic systems as a contrast between a nonegocentric and an egocentric system. Kuczaj & Maratsos (1974) also initially adopted this framework although in their conclusion they rejected it. The very language of the formulation almost necessarily leads to the prediction that the egocentric system precedes the nonegocentric one. Translating this into my terms the deictic system would precede the absolute one.

However, the formulation of the issue in terms of deictic vs. nondeictic spatial relations would lead to the opposite prediction: the absolute system will precede the deictic one. Clearly the two formulations are incompatible.

I will now try to demonstrate why the deictic system cannot be considered egocentric in a Piagetian sense. In order to be able to use the so-called 'egocentric' deictic system, the child must have decoded its use by other people, for it is only through understanding how *in back of the tree*, for example, is anchored to the position of someone else as a speaker that it is possible to use it correctly oneself. The apparent egocentrism of deictic spatial expressions depends, therefore, on a high degree of decentering. The same argument supports the contention that the deictic system is more complex than the absolute one, and the prediction that it will emerge later.

### The role of the communication matrix

The fact that this point has been neglected is symptomatic of a weakness in research on semantic development. The communication matrix in which the child's semantic system develops has often been overlooked. In communication the shifting properties of deictic expressions emerge clearly. The deictic center passes back and forth between speakers. It is not linked permanently to one individual. This is the essence of deictic phenomena. Deictic *in front of* and *in back of*, if they are egocentric for ego as speaker, are not necessarily egocentric for ego as hearer. And children who are learning to talk must operate as hearers before they can be speakers. Identifying the deictic sense of *in front of* and *in back of* as egocentric, and expecting it therefore to emerge before the absolute sense ignores these facts and treats the child's lexicon as a hermetic bubble, isolated from its sources in interaction and conversation.

At the conclusion of their paper Kuczaj & Maratsos do acknowledge that the self-referring spatial relations are not egocentric:

Egocentrism does not refer to *any* self–world relationship. Egocentrism is characterized by an inability to differentiate properly the relations between the world and the self (Piaget, 1955 [1926]). Perceiving the correct relations between oneself and objects that are involved in the use of *front* and *back* with non-fronted objects is clearly non-egocentric. (Kuczaj & Maratsos, 1974: 123)

But this acknowledgment fails to go far enough. It still ignores the fact that 'perceiving the correct relations between oneself and objects that are involved in the use of *front* and *back* with non-fronted objects' depends crucially on perceiving how these relations work in self-referring expressions used by other selves. Egocentric perception is solipsistic; but the appropriate production of self-referring deictic expressions requires the incorporation of other people's perspectives. And it is precisely because of this requirement that I would expect knowledge of the deictic system to lag behind knowledge of the absolute system.

## A study of children's comprehension of *in front of*, *in back of*, and *at the side of*

The following experiment was designed to examine children's comprehension of *in front of*, *in back of*, and *at the side of* in a situation which required a deictic interpretation of these spatial relations and in a situation which permitted an absolute interpretation. The prediction is that performance will be more advanced in the latter situation. It will be easier for children to follow the instructions when the reference object is something like a car than when it is something like a tree.

### Procedure

The experiment was divided into three sections according to the characteristics of the reference object. In one section the reference objects had an intrinsic front and back. In another section they did not. In the third section the children themselves were the reference object. Half of the children received the objects with an intrinsic front and back first, and half first received those without. All received the 'self' condition last.

The subject was seated at a small table or on the floor, with the experimenter beside him/her facing in the same direction. The experimenter handed the child a ring saying, 'I'd like you to put this ring down in certain places, and I'm going to tell you where.' The experimenter then placed a toy in front of the child and instructed: 'Put the ring in front of/in back of/at the side of the horse/boy/truck, etc.' After each placement, the experimenter removed the reference object and replaced it with another one.

Reference objects with intrinsic fronts and backs

The reference objects with intrinsic fronts and backs will be called the 'fronted' objects. Because the grounds for establishing the intrinsic fronts and backs of objects vary, and differ for animate and inanimate objects, for mobile and immobile ones, the fronted reference objects were varied across these parameters. Three were human: dolls representing a girl, a boy, and a lady. Three were animate but nonhuman: a toy horse, a toy cow, and a toy pig. Three were inanimate: a truck, a chair, and a house. All of the animate objects were mobile. The inanimate objects included one which is characteristically mobile (the truck), another which is stationary in use but can be moved (the chair), and a third which is characteristically immobile (the house).

For each of the reference objects, three placements were made, one each in front, back and side, leading to a total of twenty-seven placements. The three placements for each object were not made consecutively but were scattered at random across the sequence.

Because the objects had fronts, sides, and backs they could be placed in different orientations with respect to the subject. They could face toward him, or away from him, or sideways with respect to him. These orientations mark cardinal points. Of course the toys could also face in any direction between these points circling a full 360°. In the experiment the orientation of reference objects was varied systematically but restricted to the cardinal points. In its three presentations each object faced once towards the subject, once away and once sideways, to the left.

Orientations, placement instructions, and object features were rotated so that all possible combinations occurred exactly once, in an identical order for each child. These permutations yield twenty-seven test items. For a sample test sheet, see appendix A.

Reference objects without intrinsic fronts and backs

The objects without intrinsic fronts and backs (and sides) will be called 'frontless.' They were a bar of soap, a spool of thread, and a plastic sphere with a flattened end that allowed it to stand without rolling.

As with the fronted objects, the subjects were asked to make a total of three placements for each, a total of nine individual responses altogether. Because the objects had no front or back, they did not vary in orientation with respect to the subjects. When a spool of thread in rotated it looks essentially the same, and this condition holds for all radially symmetrical objects. A rectangular bar of soap does change is its rotations, for its long dimension can be aligned perpendicular to the child's field of vision or parallel to it. But this variation was not included as an experimental variable. The reference objects and instructions were presented to the children in a randomized order, which was identical for each child.

Half of the children received the fronted objects first, and half the frontless.

In a third section of the experiment, the children were asked to place the ring in front and in back of themselves and at their sides.

Subjects

The subjects were thirty-four middle-class children drawn from two nursery schools in Urbana, Illinois. They ranged in age from 2;6 to 5;3 and were fairly evenly distributed through this age range. No attempt was made to draw discontinuous age clusters and no a priori age groupings were made. Half the subjects were girls and half boys.

## Results and discussion

Fronted reference objects

*Cardinal points placement*. All children showed a strong orientation to the 'cardinal' directions. Whether correct or incorrect almost all placements were made in line with the two axes that divide the reference object in half, front from back and side from side. With very few exceptions (12 out of 297), placements were made directly in front, directly in back, or directly at the side rather than at intermediate points. Even children who seemed to make placements at random, or who made systematic errors, adhered to this geometry. In other words, children who show no evidence of comprehension of the prepositional expressions, *in front of*, *in back of*, and *at the side of*, reveal that they are fully aware of the planes that divide the reference objects into 'front,' 'back,' and 'sides.'

*Intrinsic feature placement.* While correct responses could theoretically be made in two different ways, either in terms of the intrinsic features of the reference objects or in terms of the spatial relation between the child and the object, children selected the former approach almost exclusively. In other words, where there was a possible ambiguity, children employed the absolute directions rather than the deictic ones. Of the fifteen children who scored 100 per cent correct, all fifteen made their placements relative to the intrinsic fronts, backs, and sides of reference objects. The errors of the other children were analyzed to see if they could be reinterpreted as correct placements in deictic terms. For the older children who only made one or two errors this did turn out to be the case. But for the younger children who made numerous errors it did not. The ratio of errors that could be interpreted as deictic placements to total errors never exceeded one-half (see table 1). For each test item, only four responses are possible. The likelihood of random responses being correct deictic placements is one-quarter for *in back of* and *in front of*, one-half for *at the side of*. The low proportion of errors interpretable as correct deictic placements to total errors does not warrant a conclusion that children who failed to apply the absolute direction system were instead applying a deictic placement strategy.

Although these results empirically undermine the view that deictic placements are more primitive than absolute placements, they do not necessarily indicate that children have a *general* tendency to choose absolute placements where possible. The results may be situationally conditioned. Deictic positions are specified with respect to a reference object and (usually) the speaker. They are more likely to be invoked when the object and the speaker are in the same 'universe.' The experimental situation, with its artificiality, and its toys that aren't for playing with, enforces a separation of universes.

*Type of reference object.* The error totals for the three categories of reference objects were 60:41:55 for human, animal and inanimate objects, respectively ($F_{2,66} = 3.197$, $p < 0.05$). However, the Scheffé

TABLE I. In front of/in back of/at the side of. *Fronted object task.*
*Proportion of errors interpretable as correct deictic placements*

| Subject (in order of increasing age) | A<br>Number of errors | B<br>Errors interpretable as deictic placements | B/A |
|---|---|---|---|
| 2 | 17 | 5 | 0.29 |
| 3 | 18 | 7 | 0.39 |
| 6 | 1 | 0 | 0.00 |
| 7 | 14 | 1 | 0.07 |
| 8 | 11 | 4 | 0.36 |
| 9 | 15 | 4 | 0.27 |
| 11 | 8 | 2 | 0.25 |
| 12 | 20 | 6 | 0.30 |
| 13 | 12 | 2 | 0.17 |
| 17 | 5 | 2 | 0.40 |
| 18 | 11 | 5 | 0.45 |
| 20 | 7 | 3 | 0.43 |
| 21 | 12 | 6 | 0.50 |
| 22 | 1 | 1 | 1.00 |
| 28 | 1 | 0 | 0.00 |
| 29 | 2 | 2 | 1.00 |
| 32 | 1 | 0 | 0.00 |
| 34 | 1 | 1 | 1.00 |
| 35 | 1 | 1 | 1.00 |

post-test does not yield significant differences between any pair of categories.

If *front, back* and *side* and the directions derived from them were learned on the basis of the child's own front, back and side, then we could expect the best performance to be with the human reference objects. However the opposite is true. In this, the third experimental setting, the children made their largest number of errors (60).

If performance were based on the kind of broad, abstract criteria that were discussed earlier as 'definitional' criteria, then we could expect performance on reference objects amenable to the same criteria to be closely related. The criteria for people and for the kinds of animals used in the experiment would presumably be direction of perception and direction of motion. On these grounds performance should be more similar when the reference object falls into these two categories than when it is an inanimate object for which the criteria for *front*, *back*, and *side* are different. Again the reverse was true. Performance with inanimate reference objects (55 errors) was intermediate between performance with human reference objects and animals (60 and 41 errors).

The fact that performance was worst with human reference objects challenges the idea that knowledge of the directions *in front of*, *in back of*, and *at the side of* is based on an extension of these directions with respect to self. The fact that performance with inanimate reference objects was intermediate between performance with two classes of animate reference objects suggests that definitional criteria such as 'direction of locomotion' or 'side receiving perceptual information' are too broad and abstract to describe how the meanings of these terms are first represented by children.

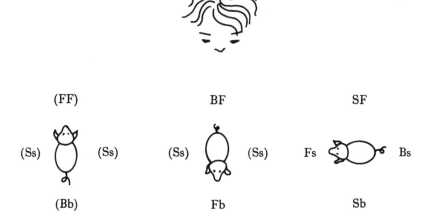

Figure 1. *In front of/in back of/at the side of*. Orientation of reference object and coordination of deictic and absolute directions
F, B, S absolute front, back, side
f, b, s deictic front, back, side
( ) deictic and absolute directions coincide

The configuration of the reference object may be an important factor. *Front/back* is the dimension of greatest extent in cows, horses and pigs. Their front end is far away from their back end. Their entire head is at their front end. People aren't built that way. Their fronts and backs are in close proximity. Perhaps this contributed to the superiority of the children's performance when the reference objects were animals.

*Orientation of reference objects.* The error totals for the three orientations of reference objects were 49:51:58 for objects facing toward, away from, and sideways with respect to the subjects, respectively. The differences are not significant ($F_{2,66} = 1.028$, $p > 0.3$).

When the reference object faced the children, the absolute and the (typical) deictic positions coincided (see figure 1). When it faced away or sideways they conflicted.

If the existence of alternative interpretations of the instructions were creating a problem for the children then one might expect better scores where the alternatives coincided, worse scores where they diverged. The face-to-face orientation does yield the lowest number of errors (49), but the difference is very small and not significant.

The results indicate that the subjects were not affected by the potential conflict in the situation. They may not have been aware of it at all. This supports the suggestion put forward above that placements were made mainly in terms of the intrinsic features of reference objects. Here we see that this system not only dominated, but seemed to suffer no competition from the alternative deictic system.

TABLE 2. In front of/in back of/at the side of. *Fronted object task. Percent errors by direction and age*

| Group[a] | Mean age (months) | Direction back | front | side | Total |
|---|---|---|---|---|---|
| 1 | 35 | 0.23 | 0.56 | 0.57 | 0.46 |
| 2 | 42 | 0.13 | 0.31 | 0.70 | 0.38 |
| 3 | 50 | 0.01 | 0.01 | 0.02 | 0.02 |
| 4 | 59 | 0.03 | 0.03 | 0.00 | 0.01 |
| Total | | 0.08 | 0.20 | 0.28 | |

[a] n = 7, 8, 9, 10, respectively.

*Age*. Older children scored better than younger ones ($F_{3,99} = 130.697$, p <0.001) (see table 2). More surprisingly there was a striking age discontinuity, with the break coming at 47 months. Below this age the mean number of errors was 10.1. Above it the mean number of errors was 0.4. Among the fifteen children in the younger group, there were three who scored one error or less. The other twelve had rather high error scores. But among the nineteen children in the older group, none had more than two errors and thirteen scored no errors. A graphic representation is the clearest way to demonstrate the age discontinuity (see figure 2).

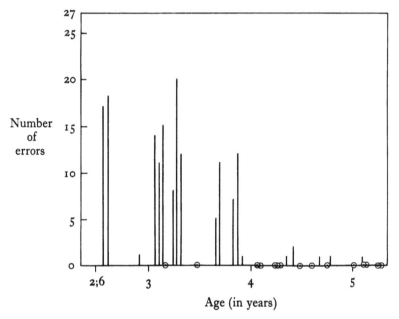

Figure 2. *In front of/in back of/at the side of.* Fronted object task. Errors by age

Harris & Strommen (1972a) reported that there was no effect of age in their data, but this was only because performance was uniformly high. Their youngest subject was 57 months old, 10 months older than the turning point in this study. Kuczaj & Maratsos (1974), whose youngest subjects were the same age as those in this experiment, do report significant improvement with age but no striking discontinuity. However, their oldest subject was 49.5 months old, only 2 months beyond the turning point. Combining these results – significant age effects below 49.5 months, no age effects above 57 months, one gets a picture that is compatible with the data of this experiment, even though the age discontinuity is not specifically replicated.

*Other variables*. An analysis of variance was done to test for effects of sex and order of presentation (fronted objects preceding or following frontless objects). Neither factor showed an effect.

## Self as reference object

The instructions to place the ring *in front of*, *in back of* and *beside* 'yourself' were given last to each child, and were apparently below the dignity of many subjects. One child refused to do it, and eight, although they complied, spontaneously and independently protested that it was 'silly.'

Each child was only asked to make one placement in each direction for a total of three with self as a reference point. Twenty-five of the thirty-three who condescended to do it were correct on all these placements; nineteen of nineteen in the older group, six of fourteen in the younger. No child who succeeded on the fronted objects task failed on the self-placement task. Three who made all the self-placements correctly failed to reach criterion on the fronted objects.

The eight errors were distributed in the amounts 0:2:6 for *front, back* and *side* instructions, respectively.

## Frontless reference objects

Scoring placements for the frontless reference objects raises some problems. One option is to treat only one type of response as correct for *in front of*: a placement on the side of the reference object nearest to the subject. *In back of* would then be the position opposite, and *at the side of* the two remaining positions (see figure 3, Pattern A).

However, there are reasons for doing the scoring in a rather different way. Some subjects were consistent in their use of a different system, in which *in front of* is on the side of the reference object that is always distant from the subject (see figure 3, Pattern B). It is as if the subject construed himself to be in line behind the reference object, and its far 'side' becomes the front of the line. This way of interpreting *in front of* and *in back of* is not restricted to children. According to Kuczaj & Maratsos (1974) a minority of adults use it too. Therefore, Pattern B

Orientation of subject

| Front | Back | Side |
|---|---|---|
| Side ◯ Side | Side ◯ Side | Back ◯ Front |
| Back | Front | Side |
| Pattern A | Pattern B | Pattern C |

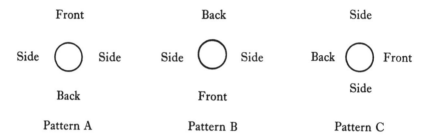

Figure 3. *In front of/in back of/at the side of.* Patterns of placement for fronted objects

cannot be treated simply as an error in the course of development, but as a genuine variant.

Hill (1978) has shown that different linguistic–cultural communities favor one pattern or the other to different degrees. Adult speakers of Hausa, for example, tend to choose Pattern B, which Hill calls the 'in-tandem prototype.' The speaker and reference object are tacitly oriented in the same direction, as if they were riding in tandem. Hill calls Pattern A, where the speaker and the reference object are tacitly face-to-face, the 'mirror-image prototype.' Experiences such as marching in line, which give rise to the in-tandem prototype, incorporate a dynamic element, while experiences such as speaking to another person or typing at a typewriter, which give rise to the face-to-face, mirror-image prototype, tend to be static. Hill shows that within the same linguistic–cultural community, different situations, highlighting dynamic or static spatial relations, promote shifts in usage from one prototype to the other.

Given these variations, it seems reasonable to credit children who apply either Pattern A or Pattern B consistently with a knowledge of the deictic system of spatial relations. And to exhaust the range of logical possibilities, there is also a Pattern C, in which *front* is to the left or right of the referent object, *back* is opposite to it, and *side* is on the near or far 'side.'

As a consequence of treating all the patterns as legitimate variants, one meets with a methodological difficulty. It is impossible to score single responses as correct or incorrect. If we assume that a child is moving toward Pattern A, 'the mirror-image prototype,' then a placement on the far 'side' of the reference object in response to *front* instructions would be incorrect; but, if he happens to be moving toward Pattern B, 'the in-tandem prototype,' then the response would be correct. It only becomes apparent which pattern children are learning if they show some degree of consistency in their responses. If responses are inconsistent, it is impossible to be certain which are correct (adult-like), and which are incorrect.

The scoring strategy I adopted takes into account the possibility that different children may systematically and not inappropriately employ different patterns. Each individual response was scored as an example of the pattern it fell into. If the instruction to put the ring in front of the thread was met with a placement on the near side of the spool, the response was scored 'A.' If the placement was on the far side of the spool, it was scored 'B.' And if it was on either of the remaining two 'sides' it was scored 'C.'

Each subject made nine responses. A string of all As indicates two things: (i) that the child had a systematic interpretation for *in front of*, *in back of*, and *at the side of* with frontless objects; (ii) that this interpretation corresponds to Pattern A. Similarly for a string of Bs or Cs. A mixture of scores indicates lack of a systematic interpretation of deictic directions.

By the strictest criterion for consistency – nine out of nine responses compatible with each other – ten children were successful. Eight employed Pattern A; two Pattern B. If the criterion is lowered to allow one inconsistent response, the number of children who were successful rises to fifteen. The ratio of pattern use in this group is 11:3:1 for Patterns A, B, and C, respectively (see table 3). All fifteen of these children fell into the older age group that emerged uniformly successful on the fronted object task. In this age group, only four children remain below criterion, and one of them had 7/9 consistent responses.

Turning now to the younger age group, three of the children showed full consistency in their responses to *back* and *front* instructions, but

TABLE 3. In front of/in back of/at the side of.
*Frontless object task. Subjects showing consistent
pattern of placements*

| Group[a] | Mean age (months) | Pattern A | B | C | Total |
|---|---|---|---|---|---|
| 1 | 35 | 1 | 0 | 1 | 2 (29%) |
| 2 | 42 | 1 | 0 | 0 | 1 (12%) |
| 3 | 50 | 4 | 1 | 1 | 6 (66%) |
| 4 | 59 | 7 | 2 | 0 | 9 (90%) |
| Total | | 13 | 3 | 2 | |

[a] n = 7, 8, 9, 10, respectively.

made incompatible responses for *side* instructions. One was among those who also scored well on the fronted objects, but the other two were not. Two of the children followed Pattern A in their *in front of* and *in back of* placements; one followed Pattern C.

These three children had learned that deictic *in back of* and *in front of* are opposite each other, but had yet to learn that *at the side of* refers to a dimension perpendicular to *in back of* and *in front of*.

All three of them happened to come from the experimental group which received fronted objects before frontless ones. This suggests the possibility that at an intermediate stage of acquisition, before the deictic system is fully elaborated, working with the nondeictic system serves a 'priming' function.

The only two children in the sample who used Pattern C showed a further internal consistency. Their *front* placements were made on the same side each time, rather than occasionally on the left, and occasionally on the right. As it happens, both of them agreed that *in front of* was on the left and *in back of* on the right side.

Comparison of performance on fronted and frontless objects

A comparison of performance on fronted and frontless objects shows that the absolute system of *in front of*, *in back of* and *at the side of* precedes the deictic one, as was predicted. In the older groups four children who reached criterion with fronted objects failed to do so with

TABLE 4. In front of/in back of/at the side of. *Subjects achieving criterion on fronted and/or frontless object tasks*

| Group[a] | Mean age (months) | Fronted object task only | Frontless object task only | Both tasks | Total fronted object task | Total frontless object task |
|---|---|---|---|---|---|---|
| 1 | 35 | 2 | 1 | 1 | 3 | 2 |
| 2 | 42 | 1 | 0 | 1 | 2 | 1 |
| 3 | 50 | 3 | 0 | 6 | 9 | 6 |
| 4 | 59 | 1 | 0 | 9 | 10 | 9 |
| Total | | 7 | 1 | 17 | 24 | 18 |

[a] n = 7, 8, 9, 10, respectively.

frontless objects. In the younger groups no child reached criterion on frontless objects, although three had done so with fronted objects.

However, the precedence of the absolute over the deictic system is not strong. In this subject population, reliable performance on both systems appears at about the same time, around 4 years. Table 4 indicates which subjects achieved criterion performance on either task alone or both tasks.

Below that age, in the younger group, three children who failed to achieve criterion on the frontless object task, did show *full* knowledge of *part* of the system. They were consistent on all *front* and *back* instructions, but made incompatible placements on *side* instructions.

The youngest of them (no. 6; aged 2;11) also met criterion on the fronted objects. The performance of subject no. 20 on fronted objects was parallel to his performance on frontless ones. He made one error in eighteen *front* and *back* placements, six errors in nine *side* placements. The third subject (no. 9) scored poorly on the fronted object task. She was the only one to perform better on frontless objects than on fronted ones. This raised the question of whether in her individual case errors on fronted objects might have been correct deictic placements. But this hypothesis failed here too, as it did in the population as a whole. Only four of her fifteen 'errors' on fronted objects could be interpreted as correct deictic placements (see table 1).

Kuczaj & Maratsos (1974), who predicted in effect that deictic placements would precede absolute ones, got results which, like those reported

TABLE 5. *Comparison of outcomes according to two methods of scoring frontless object task*

| Number of subjects reaching criterion performance on: | Kuczaj & Maratsos (1974) method of scoring (Pattern A only) | Tanz method of scoring (Patterns A, B, C) |
|---|---|---|
| Fronted and frontless objects | 12 | 17 |
| Fronted only | 12 | 7 |
| Frontless only | 1 | 1 |
| Neither | 4 | 4 |

here, show the opposite. If anything, they state this finding even more strongly and with less qualification than I find appropriate for my data. The different total impression must be due in part to differences in scoring method. Kuczaj & Maratsos treated only one pattern of response for frontless objects as correct, even though they did observe that adult patterns varied. The 'correct' pattern is the one equivalent to my Pattern A, in which the position between the reference object and the speaker is described as *in front of* the reference object. Any other pattern was scored as being wrong.

If their method of scoring were applied to my data the gap between performance on fronted objects and frontless objects would be widened. Five of the subjects who were classified as being successful on both tasks would have to be reclassified as successful on fronted objects only. Table 5 compares population profiles according to the two methods of scoring. (Subjects who scored correctly only on *front* and *back* instructions are considered to have reached criterion level performance.)

By either method of scoring a majority of the subjects achieve criterion either on both tasks or on neither, but the majority is greater by the method of scoring I used. By my method of scoring, twenty-one subjects out of twenty-nine achieve criterion on both tasks or on neither. By Kuczaj & Maratsos' method of scoring, only sixteen out of twenty-nine achieve criterion on both tasks or on neither. In other words, it yields a higher degree of correlation between success on one task and on the other.

Although the segment of the population that succeeded on only one task increases or decreases according to the method of scoring, there is no disagreement on the following: more children succeeded on the fronted object task only than on the frontless object task only. Only one subject did the reverse.

Having expected an even greater discrepancy between performance on fronted and frontless object tasks, I would like to speculate on the reasons for the narrower gap. In the discussion at the beginning of this chapter, the contrast between the two types of spatial systems was presented as dichotomous. On the one hand, there are directions based on intrinsic features of reference objects. 'In front of the car' is next to the headlight end. On the other hand, there are directions based on spatial relations between the reference object and the speaker/addressee. 'In front of the car' is between the car and the speaker. Upon re-examination in the light of the experimental results, the 'dichotomy' appears instead to be a continuous scale.

For most animate objects, it will be recalled, the front is the side that receives perceptual information or that arrives first. These criteria also apply, partly by analogy, partly directly, to many inanimate objects. For other inanimate objects (e.g. a refrigerator) the criteria have to do with user orientation or direction of access. Although these are the criteria for 'intrinsic' directions rather than for deictic ones, it can be seen that they are also relational. But the relations are of a canonical sort rather than being momentary as are deictic relations. They have to do with a user's typical orientation toward an object rather than with a speaker's particular orientation toward it at the time of speech. Therefore part of the system of intrinsic directions can be seen to have more in common with the system of deictic directions than was first evident.

This argument for continuity between the absolute and the deictic systems of spatial relations hinges on an *analytic* merger of the two systems. A second issue is empirical: to what degree are they merged in the mind of the child? If they are kept in separate compartments, then progress in one is not necessarily affected by progress *or confusion* in the other. However, if interaction does take place, then the simpler system, based on intrinsic features, can be used to stabilize the framework of the more complex system, and, conversely, confusion with regard to the more complex system may retard the final crystallization of the simpler one. In this view neither of the two sets of spatial terms can emerge in the child's lexicon if one lags behind. There seems to be no way to test the validity of this hypothesis in English. But if there were a language which lexicalized intrinsic and deictic *in front of*, *in back of*, and *at the side of* in different ways, then it could be tested. The prediction would be that the system based on intrinsic features is learned earlier than it is in English, or at least that the lag of the deictic system would be greater.

# 3 In front of *and* in back of:
## *Are they learned in backwards order?*

## Introduction

The focus of discussion so far has been on the acquisition of two complete systems of spatial relations each consisting of three directions,
*in front of, in back of,* and *at the side of.* In this section the focus will
shift to these three component directions. Are these expressions learned
simultaneously? Or does any of them precede the others? If so, why?

The theoretical framework emphasizing deixis in which the study
reported here was designed did not lead me to predict answers to these
questions, but research on the acquisition of many pairs of contrasting
relational expressions has shown that they are not learned simultaneously. And Eve Clark and Herbert Clark have formulated a general
theory to account for which member of such pairs will be learned first.
H. Clark has even offered specific predictions for the order of acquisition
of *in front of, in back of,* and *at the side of.* What follows is an evaluation
of Clark's theory, in the light of data from the experiment reported
in the previous chapter.

## A critical summary of Clark's argument on the order of acquisition of spatial terms

H. Clark (1973: 28) begins with the modest premise that 'the child
acquires English expressions for space and time by learning how to
apply these expressions to the a priori knowledge that he has about
space and time.' He then proposes that the order of acquisition of these
expressions will be determined by the 'perceptual complexity' of spatial
concepts. In the main version of his theory, he argues further that the
influence of perceptual complexity on order of acquisition is not direct,
but mediated by language itself. According to Clark, in the domain of

space, language structure reflects perceptual complexity. He tries to capture the complexity gradients on both levels, the cognitive and the linguistic, by means of feature analysis.

Clark first introduces the concept of 'perceptual space,' or space as it is cognitively structured. It might have been preferable to designate it 'conceptual space,' but perhaps Clark chooses the term 'perceptual' because he is making the point that concepts of space are constrained by the perceptual apparatus. The choice of terminology is not crucial to the argument. It is mentioned only to indicate that 'perceptual' and 'conceptual' will be used loosely in the following discussion. The term 'perceptual' will be used in direct glosses of Clark's argument, and in other contexts 'conceptual' will be used.

The basic devices that are essential for conceptualizing location in space are reference points (and their extensions – reference lines and planes), and directions. Clark goes on to argue that facts about the environment and the human organism delimit, out of all possible points of reference and directions, certain ones which are natural. Gravity is asymmetrical and defines a direction (vertical), and a plane of reference coinciding with the ground. The human body is also asymmetrical. The sensory organs, especially the eyes, are oriented more to the field in front than to the back. And normal locomotion is in a forward direction. The asymmetry of the body defines another natural direction, which for lack of a superordinate term can be called *front/back*, and a plane of reference crossing from one side to the other through the body.

Given this polarity, Clark assigns a positive value to the frontward direction and a negative value to the 'backward' direction on the grounds that everything in front is 'easily perceptible' (p. 33).

He then attempts to demonstrate that the language of spatial relations, or L-space, mirrors space as it is perceived, or P-space. Prepositional expressions specify location as a direction (the preposition) from a point of reference (the object of the preposition). One constellation of prepositions encodes the vertical direction: *up/down, above/ below, over/under, on top of/under*, etc., another encodes the front/back direction: *in front of/in back of/beside, ahead/behind, before/after*. I would not take issue with the analysis of P-space or with the analysis of L-space to this point. The claims in the section which follows are, however, questionable.

Clark now assigns positive and negative values to the linguistic poles as he has to the conceptual poles. He calls the frontward constellation of prepositions positive because *front* is 'defined in a positive way' and *ahead* is used 'metaphorically [to] indicate positive direction on a scale . . . as in John is ahead of Pete in height' (p. 43). Clark maintains that his assignment of positive and negative value to the prepositions is made purely on linguistic grounds, independently of the concepts 'back' and 'front.' The resulting match of perceptual 'front' and linguistic *front* in terms of positive and negative polarity is then treated as evidence for the isomorphism of P-space and L-space.

His predictions about the processing of prepositions in adult language comprehension and in children's acquisition of language are mediated by the facts of language structure and not, according to Clark, based directly on perceptual structure. Difficulty in processing and in acquisition is a function of the number of 'rules of application' entailed in the use of a term. Clark treats *all* negatives as requiring application of an extra rule (H. Clark, 1974). Accordingly, in his analysis the prepositions he has called negative also involve an additional rule. Therefore, they will require more processing time in adult language comprehension and, more directly at issue here, will be understood later by children. Clark reports that he has data confirming the prediction with respect to adult comprehension: verification of true and false sentences takes less time when they describe a relation between two objects X and Y as *X in front of Y* rather than *Y in back of X*. Data which bear on the prediction for acquisition order will be presented later in this chapter.

While the distinction between P-space and L-space is clear, it is questionable whether Clark's claim that he has assigned positive and negative values independently to the perceptual and linguistic polarities of 'front' and 'back' can be maintained. The idea that such assignments can be made on purely linguistic grounds is drawn from Bierwisch's (1967) discussion of German adjectives. Bierwisch develops a feature analysis for polar pairs such as *big/little, long/short, wide/narrow*, etc. He assigns positive polarity [+Pol] to the first member of each of these pairs on the grounds of examples like the following:

(1) a.   The table is twice as long as the bench.
    b.   *The table is half as short as the bench.
(2) a.   A car is half as fast as the train.
    b.   *A car is twice as slow as the train.

The b. sentences are sufficiently difficult to understand for Bierwisch to regard them as deviant. He formulates a heuristic principle of 'normality': 'A sentence is the less normal the more conditions outside of it have to be met for it to be acceptable' (p. 8). The 'normal' lexical items are positive; the 'non-normal,' negative. Positive polarity can be assigned nonarbitrarily in those adjective pairs where the two poles behave in a nonequivalent fashion. Bierwisch emphasizes that he has made the assignment on purely formal grounds. He then observes that for the adjectives he calls 'measurable' (those which can occur as parts of measure phrases, e.g. *five feet tall*), the [+Pol] feature coincides with the direction of increasing units. The fact that these adjectives indicate the extended end of a dimension is not his reason for calling them [+Pol]. Instead it is the fact that the two sets, one linguistically positive, the other cognitively positive, coincide that provides a clear instance of isomorphism between P-space and L-space.

Returning now to Clark's discussion of *in front of* and *in back of*, we will try to assess whether there are any independent formal grounds for calling the former [+Pol] and the latter [−Pol]. The problem is to discover nonequivalencies like those in examples (1) and (2) above. After much searching, I cannot discover any such discrepancies between sentences with *in front of* and *in back of*. The point is difficult to demonstrate because it doesn't depend on coming up with a counter-example to a generalization. Rather the claim is that there are no positive examples to justify the generalization to begin with. *In front of* and *in back of* might be used to describe different situations, but the situations are entirely analogous. There are no constructions that permit one to be used without allowing the other as there are some, like the measure phrases, that discriminate between *tall* and *short*.

One piece of evidence for the linguistic symmetry of the constellation of 'front' and 'back' terms, in contrast with the asymmetry of polar adjectives comes from a comparison of questions employing these terms.

While it is possible to ask either (3) or (4),

(3) How big is George?
(4) How little is George?

the questions are not symmetrical since (4) presupposes that George is relatively little, while (3) is neutral. It is also possible to ask (5) or (6):

(5) How far ahead is George?
(6) How far behind is George?

But in this case neither of the questions is neutral. They are symmetrical in that (5) presupposes that George is ahead and (6) presupposes that he is behind.

H. Clark's (1974: 43) argument that *ahead* should be [+Pol] because it 'metaphorically indicates positive direction on any scale to which it is applied' is an argument on essentially conceptual grounds. There is no linguistic asymmetry here. After all, *behind* can be used metaphorically to indicate *negative* direction on any scale to which it is applied. Sentences (7) and (8) are equally acceptable:

(7) Emma is ahead of Susan in political understanding.
(8) Susan is behind Emma in political understanding.

The property of *ahead* that Clark relies on in his argument is analogous to the property that some adjectives apply to the extended end of a dimension in that it is a semantic property. As was pointed out above, Bierwisch did not use these properties as criteria for assigning [+Pol]. On the contrary, it was after assigning polarity on linguistic grounds, that he noted its correlation with extendedness. For the adjectives, the claim that L-space preserves the structure of P-space depends crucially on treating as separate these two properties. Only then does the correlation between them demonstrate an isomorphism between L-space and P-space.

The same criticism applies to Clark's argument about why *front* should be called [+Pol]. He offers the explanation that 'it is *front* that is always defined in a positive way' (p. 43). While the generalization seems true it doesn't serve to critically distinguish *front* from *back*. *Back* can be defined in a positive way too: the *back* of a horse is the side with the tail. But even granting the point that *front* is defined in a positive way more often than *back*, the generalization reflects facts about objects in P-space directly: the fronts of objects are more salient than their backs. Clark himself bolsters his argument at this juncture by reference to the frontward direction of perception and locomotion. These are not facts about language but about objects. As linguistic entities, *front* and *back* behave in identical ways.

These arguments are not intended to challenge the designation of *front* as [+Pol] and *back* as [−Pol], but only to point out that if such a feature assignment is made, it is made entirely on conceptual grounds and not on independent linguistic grounds as Clark has claimed. It still makes sense to speak of distinct levels, 'front' and 'back' in P-space, and *front* and *back* in L-space. But in this case it turns out that L-space *fails* to preserve an important aspect of P-space. There are no non-arbitrary linguistic grounds for assigning the feature [+Pol] to *front*.

While it is still a viable distinction in general, the distinction between P-space and L-space collapses in the context of Clark's predictions for language comprehension and language acquisition. Since there is no longer any basis for saying that *front* is linguistically positive, claims about its relative ease of processing must be made purely on conceptual grounds. If Clark's experiments did show faster reaction times for confirming sentences with *in front* than for those with *in back*, the explanation should be formulated in terms of conceptual 'positiveness' instead of linguistic 'positiveness.'

At the end of his paper, Clark does admit the possibility that the order of acquisition of spatial terms may be governed directly by perceptual complexity, and not mediated by linguistic complexity. But he considers this a possibility only under special circumstances: if children have not fully mapped out conceptual space when they begin to learn spatial terminology, then their first terms will necessarily relate to their first concepts. This second model, then, proposes that concepts receive labels as they become consolidated. If, on the other hand, the conceptual system is fully consolidated before the beginning of the acquisition of spatial terms, then order is governed by the mediating factor of linguistic complexity, which reflects perceptual complexity. This is the original model discussed in detail above. According to Clark, both models make the same prediction: *in front of* will be learned before *in back of*.

Clark also makes the prediction that *beside* or *at the side of* will be learned later than the *front* and *back* prepositions. He follows Bierwisch (1967) in his analysis of spatial adjectives in terms of the number of dimensions they presuppose. *Long* and *short* presuppose a single dimension; *wide* and *narrow* presuppose two. Each dimension presupposed is represented as an additional feature in the feature specification of the adjective. Clark's contribution is the argument that each feature adds an increment of difficulty in processing. *In front of* and *in back of* presuppose only one dimension, length. *At the side of* presupposes a second, width. Therefore, *at the side of* is more complex, and should be the last to be acquired.

# Experimental results[1]

An age group (4) × direction (3) × orientation (3) × object (3), repeated measures ANOVA was carried out on the data. The main effects for age ($F_{3,99} = 130.697$, p <0.001), direction ($F_{2,66} = 33.951$, p <0.001), and object ($F_{3,99} = 3.197$, p <0.040) were significant.

## At the side of

Subjects made more errors in response to *at the side of* instructions than either *in front of* or *in back of* instructions (p <0.05, Student–Newman–Keuls test, see table 2). This was the case despite the fact that the chance of a random placement being correct is twice as high for *side* instructions as for *front* and *back* instructions.

## In front of vs. in back of

Scores for *in front of* vs. *in back of* were also significantly different (p < 0.01, Scheffé test, see table 2). However, the direction of the difference was opposite to that predicted by Clark. Children performed better on *in back of* instructions than *in front of* instructions.

Grouping the data in this way does not report the effects as strongly as they could be reported. It is instructive to look at the patterns of scoring child by child. For this analysis we will concentrate on the younger group of subjects rather than the older ones, none of whom made more than two errors. Among the fifteen children in the younger group, not one made more errors on *in back of* instructions than *in front of*. And five scored perfectly on *in back of* while still making errors on *in front of*. In other words, there was not a single case of consolidation of the meaning of *in front of* while the interpretation of *in back of* remained in fluctuation.

This method of scrutinizing data would seem to be applicable in many studies of semantic development. Results are commonly reported for groups of subjects. If responses for one term, for example *big*, are correct significantly more often than responses for *little*, the conclusion is drawn that children learn *big* before *little*. The import of this conclusion must vary, however, according to whether only a majority learn *big* before *little* and a minority *little* before *big*, or whether all children uniformly learn *big* before *little*.

[1] Data from the fronted object task are described in chapter 2.

In the section of the experiment employing frontless reference objects, children showed an asymmetry of response which may have contributed to the pattern of results for fronted reference objects. 'Correct' responses to *at the side of* instructions were distributed unevenly between right side and left side, the right side being preferred at a ratio of 2:1. The way this asymmetry may have influenced results for fronted objects is as follows. It will be recalled that one variable in the fronted object experiment was the direction in which the reference object was facing. When the object faced directly toward or away from the child, the sideways asymmetry of response could have no influence on *in front of* and *in back of* scores. However, in the third orientation, when the reference object faced sideways, it could be presumed to have an effect because the reference object always faced toward one side, the left. The correct response for *in front of* instructions was a placement on the left side; for *in back of* instructions, it was on the right. Therefore, in random responding the chance of making a correct placement for *in back of* instructions is twice as high as it is for *in front of* instructions.

To correct for this unexpected artifact, the test items where the reference object faced sideways were eliminated and the data were re-analyzed. Responses to *in back of* instructions were still correct significantly more often than responses to *in front of* ($p < 0.01$, Sign test, 2-tail).

Kuczaj & Maratsos (1974), expecting that *in front of* would precede *in back of*, report that instead they found the two expressions were learned simultaneously. This contradicts the findings reported here, but the difference may be traceable to an artifact of Kuczaj & Maratsos' experimental procedure. They gave their subjects the three instructions for each reference object consecutively. The order of the instructions was varied, but the fact that they were presented consecutively, given the demand characteristics of the situation, might have crucially influenced the children to change their response for each new instruction (direction). More specifically, if children have absorbed the fact that whatever *in back of* and *in front of* actually mean, they mean the opposite of each other – then their responses will not be independent. Say, for example, that the first instruction in a sequence is *in back of*. If children make a correct placement in this case, then when *in front of* is required they make the opposite placement and are correct again. On the other hand, if they are wrong on their first placement then they are likely to be wrong again if they respond to the opposite instruction by moving their marker to the opposite side. Under these circumstances, the experiment artificially causes scores for *in back of* and *in front of* to converge.

It would be possible to test this interpretation of Kuczaj & Maratsos' results by analyzing their data in the following way: compare the number of correct responses in triplets of instructions when the first one requires an *in front of* placement, and when it requires an *in back of* placement. The prediction is that there will be more correct responses for both *in back of* and *in front of* when the *in back of* instruction is given first.[1]

## Discussion

### At the side of

Clark's semantic feature hypothesis correctly predicted that *at the side of* would be learned last. But in order to evaluate the results as broadly as possible it might be worthwhile considering other factors that could have contributed to them, especially in light of the failure of the semantic feature hypothesis to make correct predictions for which of these relations would be learned first.

One factor may well have been the uncommonness of the expression *at the side of*. It was chosen, instead of the more common, *beside*,[2] for its parallelism with *in front of* and *in back of*. Another factor is that the nominal source of this prepositional phrase, *side* itself, can be used in a directionally neutral way. A box, for example, may be described as having two sides, four, or six; if four or six, then the sides are not being distinguished from the front and back. Even when the direction is specified, the face of an object can still be called a *side*, as in the *front side* of a house. Although this flexibility does not extend to the phrase, *at the side of*, in adult language, it may be mistakenly overgeneralized by children.

To decide whether the number-of-dimensions hypothesis is a satisfactory explanation for the result it successfully predicted, it will

[1] I have proposed this analysis to Maratsos and he has kindly carried it out. He reports (personal communication) that there was no difference 'looking at *front* and *back* separately when first received by the children.'

[2] Jones & Wepman (1966) include *beside* in their list of the most common prepositions in spoken English. The criterion they used is appearance in the speech of at least two subjects out of 54 sampled over 10,000-word segments of speech. *Side* does not appear on the list; therefore its phrasal derivatives *at the side of* and *by the side of* can be assumed to be less common.

probably be necessary to test other closely related predictions. Clark has analyzed the prepositions *at, on,* and *in* as presupposing one, two, and three spatial dimensions, respectively.

An auxiliary question should therefore be asked: do children actually master *at* before *on,* and both before *in?* Summaries of early language give the impression that the answer is no. Brown (1973) reports that *in* and *on* are the first locative prepositions to appear in spontaneous speech. And E. Clark (1972b) offers experimental evidence that comprehension of *in* precedes comprehension of *on.* She interprets her findings in terms of greater perceptual saliency for the young child of containers than of surfaces. In sum, the order of acquisition of the prepositions seems to be exactly the reverse of what would be predicted by H. Clark's hypothesis: *in, on, at* instead of *at, on, in.* His proposal was that each dimension required to specify the meaning of a term corresponds to one semantic feature and that each increment of features contributes to difficulty in acquisition. If the proposal fails in this case, its applicability to *at the side of* becomes questionable, even though the prediction that emerged from it was correct.

### In front of vs. in back of

Assuming with Clark, as it seems reasonable to do, that *front* is the perceptually positive direction, we must conclude that perceptual positiveness does not absolutely govern the order of language acquisition. It is clear, as Clark argues, that children must have mapped out a conceptual domain before they can master the language related to it. But they need not precisely duplicate the sequence in which they first explored and staked out the territory when they learn to talk about it. The thesis that they do exactly duplicate their steps seems to regard children as though they were learning language in isolation – dipping into the communal pot of the language only to draw out labels for concepts each has arrived at alone. Reiterating the criticism advanced in the last chapter, what is neglected in the study of language acquisition is the communication matrix, which sets up priorities that interact with perceptual positiveness to determine the order of acquisition of terms.

How does the communication matrix select *in back of* to be learned before *in front of?* Admittedly the answer proposed below is post hoc and unsystematic, but a systematic prior analysis depends upon a theory of communication that does not yet exist.

*In back of* and *in front of* are used to describe sequences of two or more objects. When we describe a sequence we usually identify one object as being first. We can do it in such a way that the other object is *in back of it* or, choosing a different object as the first, the other is *in front of it*. Perceptual salience selects the point of reference. Other things being equal, it will be the front-most object. Then it will follow that the other object is construed as being in back of it. Therefore, even though *front* is perceptually positive, and in this case *because* it is perceptually positive, *in back of* is highlighted in communication. This argument rests on the fact that there are variations in *how* a certain piece of information can be expressed, and that some ways communicate more effectively than others. A different point rests on the issue of *when* certain types of information are required. When we consider the multiplicity of occasions for using locative expressions, it seems plausible that on balance it is more often when some object is not immediately perceptible to an addressee. This is more likely to be the case when the object is hidden in back of something than in full view in front of it. Then of necessity, rather than by strategic choice, the point of reference will be an object that is in front and the object that is the focus of discussion will be described as being in back of it.

For both reasons one would expect *in back of* to be used more frequently in spoken language, and this is in fact the case. Jones & Wepman (1966) list all words occurring above a minimum level of frequency in the speech of fifty-four speakers describing TAT cards, or appearing in the speech of at least two of these subjects. Of the words *front*, *back*, and *side*, only *back* appears on the list of most frequent prepositions. *Behind*, essentially synonymous, also turns up. Given two objects A and B we are more likely to talk first about A and then *B behind A* than first about B and then *A in front of B*.

It could then be argued that frequency alone determines the order of acquisition. But numerous studies have shown that frequency per se is an unreliable predictor. E. Clark (1972a) has argued persuasively that where frequency does correlate with order, it fails to predict patterns of error and substitution. Frequency should be considered rather an epiphenomenon, variously reflecting the interplay of syntactic, conceptual and pragmatic factors in speech production and language acquisition.

To reiterate and expand the point made above, *in back of* will be highlighted in communication because there will be more occasions when it is required, and because even when it is not required it will tend to have greater communicative value. This is not to say that children learn it first because they are trying to maximize their communicative currency and therefore acquire terms that possess greater value. But expressions that communicate clearly will be comprehended more readily by children, and for that reason will be acquired earlier.

### Other terms incorporating the front–back dimension

*Push/pull.* If the results of this experiment on *in front of* and *in back of* disconfirm the predictions of H. Clark's feature hypothesis, what of other sets of terms that also incorporate the front–back dimension? Data on the acquisition of at least two such sets of terms exist in the literature. One is the pair of motion verbs, *push* and *pull*; the other is the pair of temporal adverbs, *before* and *after*.

In a study by Huttenlocher, Eisenberg & Strauss (1968) children were asked to make one truck push another or pull another, or, alternatively, be pushed or pulled by another. H. Clark reasons that *push* 'implies the locative' *in back of* (presumably because the agent is in back of the object); conversely *pull* implies *in front of*. Therefore, he says he would have predicted *pull* to be learned more readily than *push*. Huttenlocher et al. show the opposite to be true. *Push* is learned before *pull*. In order to incorporate these results, Clark revises his analysis of *push* and *pull*, and now proposes that in their most general sense,

> *push* means to 'move in a forward direction from the agent' [note the un-acceptability of *\*John pushed it toward himself*] whereas *pull* means to 'move in a backward [vis-à-vis the agent] direction towards the agent' [note the unacceptability of *\*John pulled it away from himself*, at least without odd contrivances] . . . *Push* and *pull*, therefore, contain the meanings, *move forward* and *move backward*. (1974: 1358; Clark's brackets)

On the basis of this revised analysis, Clark comes to the qualified conclusion that the *push/pull* data support his prediction.

The revised analysis of *push* and *pull* is confusing at best. With a stationary agent, to *push* does mean to move an object in a direction away from the agent, and to *pull*, in a direction toward the agent, but why forward versus backward? *Toward* and *away from* seem to capture the distinction adequately.

With an agent that is in motion, the direction of motion is simply the direction in which the agent is moving. The agent of *push* may be moving either forward or backward, facing in the direction of motion or away from it, and likewise for the agent of *pull*. It's true that if one puts the cart before the horse, then the horse can only push, but this is a restriction that applies to horses and not to pushing or pulling.

A person can push a door while facing it, or as in the case of a waiter with his arms full, while leaning into the door with his posterior. A puller can pull a kite while running forward to keep an eye on the terrain or running backward to keep an eye on the kite. Like the agent, the object can be moving either forward or backward with respect to its own orientation or the orientation of the agent. The single systematic distinction between pushers and pullers is that a pusher is behind the object with respect to the direction of motion, and a puller must be ahead of it. And this brings us back full cycle to Clark's original analysis, relating *push* to *in back of* and *pull* to *in front of*.

If either of two opposing interpretations of the semantics of *push* and *pull* could be maintained with equal plausibility, then this pair of terms would not be a suitable one for testing the predictions of the feature hypothesis. But if one interpretation is to be preferred over another, and I believe it should be, it is Clark's original interpretation which makes *push* analogous with *in back of* and *pull* with *in front of*. The Huttenlocher et al. finding that *push* is learned before *pull* then reverses Clark's feature hypothesis predictions. But it is precisely compatible with the finding reported here that *in back of* is learned before *in front of*.

Unfortunately, the explanation offered earlier in this chapter for the priority of *in back of* over *in front of* is not broad enough to cover *push* and *pull*. The congruence of the two sets of findings invites speculation about the existence of some more general principle that does.

*Before/after.* The spatial relations *in front of* and *in back of* have a metaphorical extension in the domain of time. In fact, as H. Clark points out, all relational prepositions of time in English are derived from them: *before, after, ahead, behind*, etc. According to his general hypothesis, children should learn *before* before *after*, and he cites E. Clark (1971) for evidence that in fact they do. E. Clark's central explanation for her results is derived from H. Clark's theory. *Before* is simpler than *after* because the meaning of *after* is represented with an additional negative feature:

(9) *before*:   + Time
                − Simultaneous
                + Prior
(10) *after*:   + Time
                − Simultaneous
                − Prior                                    (E. Clark, 1971 : 273)

Amidon & Carey (1972) have challenged her interpretation on the ground that in their experiment children successfully follow commands involving the temporal terms *first* and *last. First* and *last* also mark the distinction [±Prior], and therefore the presence of this feature alone cannot explain the delay in learning *before* and *after*.

What can explain the delay, and why is it greater for *after* than for *before*? Amidon & Carey offer an answer to the first of these questions. *Before* and *after* sentences place an extra-syntactic demand upon the child, requiring him to coordinate a main clause and a subordinate clause. Instructions with *first* and *last* are conjunctions of two main clauses.

There is a corollary to this structural difference that Amidon & Carey do not mention. Each of the commands in their experiment on *first* and *last* incorporated both of these terms, for example *Move a red plane first; move a blue plane last. Before* and *after* instructions include either one or the other term, for example *Move a red plane before you move a blue plane*, or *Move a blue plane after you move a red plane*. In other words, in the Amidon & Carey experiment, where sequencing information is provided by using *first* and *last*, each clause carries its own temporal tag, making the temporal information redundant across clauses.

As for the second question, pertaining to the lag between acquisition of *before* and *after*, E. Clark herself, presenting an alternative to the feature hypothesis, offers an explanation that is compatible with Amidon & Carey's objection. Two factors converge in her explanation. The first is that, for English-speaking children, sentences with the subordinate clause following the main clause are easier to process than those with the subordinate clause preceding. The second is that sentences which are iconic, or preserve the temporal order of events, are easier for children to comprehend than those which reverse the order of events. In some sentences with *before*, the easier values of both of these variables coincide (see sentence (11)). They never do in sentences with *after* (see sentences (13) and (14)).

|  | Main clause first | Iconic |
|---|:---:|:---:|
| (11) He jumped the gate before he patted the dog. | + | + |
| (12) Before he patted the dog, he jumped the gate. | − | − |
| (13) He patted the dog after he jumped the gate. | + | − |
| (14) After he jumped the gate, he patted the dog. | − | + |

For this reason the meaning of a sentence like (11) is the most likely to be grasped when the child hears it in speech, and the meaning of the word *before* learned in this facilitating context.

By the account presented above, the precedence of *first* and *last* over *before* and *after* is due to a syntactic factor. The precedence of *before* over *after* in their function as subordinating conjunctions is due to the joint operation of a syntactic and a semantic factor.

E. Clark's original formulation of the syntactic factor which favors *before* was stated in terms of the greater 'derivational simplicity' of sentences in which the main clause precedes the subordinate clause. The concept of derivational simplicity originates in transformational grammar and pertains to the sequence of transformational steps employed in generating a sentence. All other things being equal, a sentence with fewer transformations is considered derivationally simpler than one with more. In some analyses of English, the order, main clause first, subordinate clause second, is considered basic and the process of moving the subordinate clause to the front of a sentence is seen as adding a transformational step. At the time of Clark's writing, derivational simplicity was thought to be a predictor of ease of processing in adults and ease of acquisition in children. Subsequent research undermined this idea as a general claim. But the 'derivational simplicity' hypothesis aside, research tends to support the idea that for English-speaking children, it is easier to comprehend and produce sentences in which the main clause precedes the subordinate clause.

So far, then, two different syntactic factors have been suggested as possibly interacting with the semantic factor of iconicity to produce various contexts for interpreting *before* and *after*: the order of main and subordinate clauses, and derivational simplicity. There are yet other ways of construing the syntactic factor. Menn (personal communication)

T ABLE 6. Before *and* after *as subordinating conjunctions in sentence structures varying iconicity, clause order, and conjunction position*

| Order of events: A B | | | |
|---|---|---|---|
| Order of clauses; position of conjunction | Iconic | Main clause first | Conjunction central |
| Languages with clause-initial conjunctions (e.g. English) | | | |
| 1. A (*before* B) | + | + | + |
| 2. B (*after* A) | − | + | + |
| 3. (*before* B) A | − | − | − |
| 4. (*after* A) B | + | − | − |
| Languages with clause-final conjunctions (e.g. Japanese) | | | |
| 5. A (B *before*) | + | + | − |
| 6. B (A *after*) | − | + | − |
| 7. (B *before*) A | − | − | + |
| 8. (A *after*) B | + | − | + |

has suggested a 'conjunction position' factor. The subordinating conjunctions *before* and *after* can occur either between the two clauses in a central position, or in a 'marginal' position outside the two clauses (see table 6, lines 1, 2, 7, 8, and lines 3, 4, 5, 6, respectively).

Menn speculates that it might be easier for children to discover that the conjunction serves a linking function when it is positioned between two clauses than when it is positioned outside. In English this constraint combined with the iconicity principle would also favor *before* over *after* since it is *before* which can be simultaneously central and iconic (see line 1). This analysis could be subjected to a cross-language test by examining what happens in languages with clause-final conjunctions (e.g. Japanese). In such languages iconicity and central position of the conjunction will coincide in expressions with *after* (see line 8). These expressions happen to have the subordinate clause preceding. By the conjunction position hypothesis, children learning such languages should master *after* as a subordinating conjunction before they master *before*. By the clause order hypothesis, they should still master *before* first.

Japanese does not provide an ideal test case because, as it happens, Japanese *always* places the subordinate clause first. It permits only the forms in lines 7 and 8 of table 6. It excludes the forms in lines 5 and 6.

Whether *before* is used, or *after*, the conjunction is always central, and the main clause is always last. So these two principles cannot be pitted one against the other. However, Japanese would still provide an interesting opportunity to investigate the contribution of iconicity to decoding *before* and *after*. In Japanese, it is sentences with *after* that preserve the actual order of events (see line 8). But the ideal general test case would only be provided by a language with clause-final conjunctions in which the order of the clauses can vary.

To make matters even more complicated, there is some controversy about the basic facts to be explained. E. Clark concluded that children understood the meaning of *before* before *after* on the basis of children's performance with two-clause sentences. Bowerman (1979) reviews other studies which question this interpretation stating that children may already know the meanings of the words in simpler contexts but be hampered by the two-clause constructions. Coker (1975), for example, found that 5 and 6 year old children who made errors when acting out sentences in which *before* and *after* served as subordinating conjunctions were able to respond correctly to questions like *What did I show you before/after the X?*, and Coker & Legum (1974) found that while some children learned *before* first, others learned *after*. However, Harner (1976) has presented data that corroborate those of E. Clark if Clark's are interpreted narrowly rather than broadly. In her studies *before* is easier for children to understand than *after* when it introduces a subordinate clause, but not necessarily in other contexts. It is therefore possible that even if overall claims about the order of acquisition of *before* before *after* were untenable, the data might support generalizations about them in specific roles such as subordinating conjunction. If this is the case, explanations will still be necessary, and the views advanced above concerning interactions between iconicity, on the one hand, and clause order and conjunction position, on the other, may be significant in the analysis of the new, narrower problem.

Reviewing the pairs of terms whose meaning incorporates the *front/back* distinction, we see that H. Clark's feature hypothesis has failed to predict the order of acquisition within two: *in front of/in back of*, *push/pull*. For the third, *before/after*, the prediction may be partially correct, but in the light of the Amidon & Carey (1972) experiment, and the failure on *in front of/in back of*, it seems that factors, both syntactic and semantic, other than those captured in a feature analysis of word meaning explain the results better.

*Some afterthoughts on the 'before' and 'after' studies.* In both the E. Clark (1971) and the Amidon & Carey (1972) experiments children's comprehension of the terms *before* and *after* may be underestimated. The subjects are required to process sentences that offer syntactic obstacles to comprehension. Even if they do understand the sentences, they need to be able to remember the order of the events described by rote memory. The logic of the experiments requires using sequences of events whose order is arbitrary and reversible. To tap children's earliest knowledge of *before* and *after* such obstacles should be removed, perhaps by questioning them about the order of events in real-life circumstances where temporal order has significance. For example:

(15) What do you do before you come to school?
(16) What do you do after you come to school?
(17) Do you eat dessert before or after dinner?

Through these questions, comprehension of *before* and *after* would be isolated from comprehension of sentences with subordinate clauses and from memory for the order of arbitrarily ordered events. Coker's (1975) questions, for example, *What did I show you before/after I showed you the X?*, approximate these in form but still require children to commit to memory a novel sequence of events/pictures. Admittedly some of the questions above have subordinate clauses themselves, but here the problem of correctly relating the information in the subordinate clause and in the main clause seems to be reduced, partly because the information in the main clause is itself reduced.

In general there is something to be said for testing children's comprehension by talking to them rather than just by making them carry out instructions. 'Comprehension tests' in language acquisition research have come to be restricted largely to scenarios in which the experimenter says something and the subjects *do* something. There is nothing inherently necessary in this paradigm. It may be that it is an inheritance from the early days of language acquisition studies when the focus of research was more exclusively on syntax. Questions probing syntax often require meta-linguistic judgments for answers and are notoriously difficult to administer to children. To probe semantic development it is not necessary to ask questions directly about language but only about general information, and then to infer from the answers how the terms of the questions were understood.

# 4 *Personal pronouns*

## Introduction: failure to use personal pronouns

Some children fail to use personal pronouns in their earliest speech. The aspect of this phenomenon that has been noted most often is children's use of their names to refer to themselves. Correlated with this (but less often remarked in a literature that has focused on the first uses of *I* as evidence of the emergence of the concept of 'self') is children's use of a name to refer to the person they are addressing.

In the multi-lingual collection of mother–child dialogues that forms the data base for Brown's *A first language* (1973), references to self and to mother constitute a large proportion of words occurring in early combinatorial utterances. The term 'pivot' has been used to designate words which occur with high frequency in initial two-word sentences and in combination with many other words in a child's vocabulary. Terms referring to self appear among the four most frequent pivots for 8 of 17 children; terms referring to mother appear for 7 of 17. For 5 out of the 8, the term referring to self is the proper name. For all 7 out of the 7, the term referring to mother is *mommy*.

The preferred forms of self-reference and addressee reference vary from culture to culture, for adults as well as for children. In Polish, for example, it is entirely proper to refer to the addressee in the third person, using a proper name. In fact second-person address is restricted to people who are on familiar terms. But in the English exchanged between adults, third-person addressee reference and third-person self-reference are not standard. Yet here are some examples of this type of usage from dialogues with Adam and Eve:

(1) (2;1) Eve: Eve lunch.
         Mother: Eve's having lunch.
(2) (2;3) Eve: Mommy stool.
         Mother: Yes, mommy's sitting on the stool.

(3)        Adam: Adam busy.
           Mother: Adam's busy? What is Adam busy doing?
           Adam: I'm busy at home.
           Mother: You're busy at home?

These examples also illustrate the fact that the use of proper name reference for speaker and addressee is not restricted to children but is present in the speech of parents. It may indeed be a fairly typical characteristic of adult baby-talk.

In one impressive sequence, Eve's mother runs through the repertoire of all possible forms of reference to her addressee, her daughter:

(4) Is *Eve* tired?
    *She* is.
    Would *you* like to go to bed?
    All right. *We*'ll go to bed.

The only imaginable pronominal alternative that is not included is one that is not acceptable in English anyway, but is apparently common in Japanese. Japanese parents address a male child as *boku* which is an informal term for *I* or *me*. In other words they freeze the first-person pronoun and use it as a form of address for the child (Fischer, 1964).

## Self-reference and addressee reference in motherese

Why do parents use proper names to refer to themselves and to the child they are addressing? It may be that they introduce them intuitively as a device to simplify communication. Names make the identification of referents more specific and explicit than do variable pronouns. And although this is probably a side-effect, exclusion of the first and second persons also narrows the range of verb forms and keeps them more uniform.

A very different kind of explanation for this attribute of 'motherese' derives from a sociolinguistic perspective on communication. Cicourel (1970: 147), in making the point that linguistic competence is not sufficient for communicative interaction, argues that there are other 'interpretive procedures' involved in making sense of events and utterances. One such 'procedure' is the assumption of 'reciprocity of perspectives': 'the member's idealization of the interchangeability of standpoints whereby the speaker and hearer both take for granted . . . that each . . . would probably have the same experience of the immediate scene if they were to change places'; and the corollary: 'that members assume and assume others assume it of them, that their descriptive accounts or utterances will be intelligible and recognizable features of a world known in common and taken for granted.'

Young children, and especially infants, violate these basic assumptions. They don't understand fully. They can't reply fully. The mutually acknowledging, reciprocal *I/you* system may seem somehow inappropriate to the parents in this situation. They resort to the third person instead.

This effect might be comparable to another which makes it possible to refer to babies as *it*, in apparent violation of rules for pronominalizing referents that are animate and human. If the sex of an adult is unknown, he or she has been referred to as *he*, at least prior to the feminist revolt against this usage. In any case, an animate pronoun is used. But even if the sex of a baby is known, it may still be referred to as *it*, and if its sex is unknown, it is most likely to be referred to as *it*.

Very old people, sick people, or people in subordinate positions, may also be subject to nonstandard forms of address. A doctor might say to a patient, *How are we today?* A teacher might say to a student, *How did we do on that test last week?* A literal reading of these expressions would suggest that the speakers feel solidarity with the addressees, assuming their points of view with regard to health, or performance on the test. But, as everyone knows, the attitude actually communicated is one of distancing.[1] The speakers are being patronizing to the addressees. Perhaps the vehicle of such messages is the speakers' reluctance to use a reciprocal form of address. *I/you* is reciprocal. *We* is not. If the addressee assimilates it to reciprocal exchange by replying, for example, *We passed, thank you*, he communicates that he was offended and that he is willing to offend in return.

Although third-person self- and addressee reference is a common characteristic of American motherese, it is not clear that children learn it from their parents. Some may adopt it spontaneously. The question can only be resolved by studying the beginnings of self- and addressee

---

[1] D. McNeill (personal communication) has pointed out that there is some affiliative residue in this usage since it does not extend to genuinely antagonistic relations. Consider the unlikelihood of:

Policeman: We were speeding, weren't we?

or

Mugger: Do we have some money today?

(McNeill's examples)

reference in children, and by studying parental speech to them from a very early age, long before the onset of speech in the children.

## Failure to 'shift' personal pronouns

When children do begin to use personal pronouns, they sometimes produce errors involving failure to shift. Brown's Adam demonstrates this in the following sequence (age 2;6):

(5) Adam: Fell down mommy.
  Mother: You fell down?
  A: Yeah.
  M: Did you hurt yourself?
  A: Yeah.
  M: What did you hurt?
  A: Hurt your elbow.

Judging from his mother's reply, he apparently makes the reciprocal error in the first phrase in this example (age 3;2):

(6) Adam: Hit my knee.
  Mother: Hit *my* knee.
  Adam: Hit your knee.

What is striking here is how readily he grasps his mother's correction, despite the fact that word-for-word it duplicates his incorrect remark.

The only case I have encountered of *over*-application of shifting is one of a small boy who refused to recite the alphabet. He had been laughed at once when, after successfully getting through the first twenty-two letters, he had ended with 'V, double-me, X,Y,Z.'

Semantic person and syntactic person

Huxley's (1970) subject, Douglas, exhibited an interesting strategy for acquisition of *I* exemplified as follows:

(7) (2;3–2;7) Douglas empty that out.
(8) (2;7)   I, Douglas picks up big cards on floor.
(9) (3;1)   I want a sweet, Douglas want a sweet.

First he used only his name. Then he introduced the pronoun in combination with the name. Finally he 'practiced' by substituting one for the other in a single, paradigmatic sentence frame.

In parental speech the third person for self or addressee is accompanied by all the third-person syntactic reflexes – verb agreement, etc. It is interesting to note Douglas' usage in this respect. In example (7) the verb does not agree with the third-person form of the subject. It can be construed either as agreeing with the subject on semantic grounds (the subject is the speaker and therefore first person), or as being un-marked, or as echoing a second-person command made to Douglas by someone else. The fragment from her corpus of Douglas' speech that Huxley includes in her published text does not permit a choice between these three interpretations, since there is neither positive evidence that he ever uses the third-person verb inflection at this stage in his development nor negative evidence that he fails to do so, and no discourse context is provided.

Example (8) comes from a period in which Douglas sometimes used *I* alone, sometimes *Douglas* alone, and sometimes, as in the example, both in combination. On each occasion of using *I* alone, the verb agrees with *I*. When *Douglas* is used, agreement is sometimes third-person (e.g. *Douglas leaves on my shirt*) as in (8), sometimes first-person (e.g. *Douglas eat all my sweets*).

Example (9) comes from a period in the sample when third-person agreement had already been demonstrated. So here the absence of third-person present verb marking *can* be interpreted as first- or second-person rather than as neutral. In the repetition of sentence frames in example (9) the verb form does not change in concord with the subject. Agreement remains with the first person. Judging from the published sample, it appears that this type of usage is the last occurrence of proper name self-reference. Thereafter, Douglas used first-person pronouns. It is interesting to speculate that the first-person agreement in examples such as (9) reflects a late stage in the emergence of first-person semantics, after which the proper name can be dropped.

The agreement of the verb with the semantic rather than the syntactic person is delineated even more clearly for the copula and for auxiliary uses of *be*. There is evidence that Douglas correctly assigned *am* to the first-person pronoun and *is* to the third-person pronoun (with a third-person referent) by the age of 3;0:

(10) (2;9) Look where I'm running.
          I am taking my shoes off.
     (3;0) Him is driver.
     (3;1) There is him carrying paint.

Yet at 3;1, Douglas also produces the following sentence, at once an affirmation of identity and first-personhood.

(11) (3;1) Douglas am Douglas Scott Brown.

Although the subject is syntactically third-person, the verb agreement is clearly first-person.

   Example (12), a common form in Douglas' speech at age 3, involves a combination of persons that appears to be excluded in adult speech.

(12) Douglas eat all my sweets . . .

An adult would be syntactically consistent within a clause. If he referred to himself in the third person once, he would do it twice, as in example (13a), and would never utter (13b).

(13) (Hypothetical)
    a. Daddy: Daddy hurt his hand.
    b. Daddy: Daddy hurt my hand.

Douglas sometimes repeats the third-person self-referential term as a noun (cf. (14)), but never as a third-person pronoun.

(14) Douglas get sting if Douglas pull up nettles . . .

   Therefore, in setting up congruence, whether between subject and verb, or subject and coreferential pronoun, Douglas adheres to a semantic 'concept' of person, rather than a syntactic one.


Alienable names

Examination of some of the well-known corpora in the child language literature suggests the hypothesis that around the time that children who have used the proper name to refer to themselves graduate to using pronouns, the topic of self-reference engages their conscious attention. Eve and Adam both indulge in jokes about their names:

(15) Eve: Eve name Linda.
    Mother: Your name isn't Linda. Your name's what?
    Eve: Eve name 'red bicycle.'
    Mother: 'Red bicycle?' She was 'tomato juice' the other night.
(16) Adam: I not spaghetti.
    Mother: You're not spaghetti? What are you?
    Adam: I'm Adam.

Adam's gags appear in the protocol immediately following one where he announces: 'I Adam.' For Huxley's Douglas, the pronouncement that 'Douglas am Douglas Scott Brown' precedes by about one month the completion of the long transition to using $I$ instead of his name.

This toying with identities and referential tags may reflect a variety of preoccupations. A more complete examination of corpora would be required to discover whether it is correlated with the adoption of the 'alienable' pronouns as terms of reference for self and addressee.

### Speaker/hearer indexing

Even when the personal pronouns are present in child speech, the speaker/hearer indexing properties of $I$ and $you$ may not have been activated. In a detailed study of the emergence of $I$ and $you$ in Eve's speech, McNeill (1963) argued that although her use of these pronouns appeared to be correct on the surface, she was not actually using them to refer to the deictic coordinates of 'speaker' and 'hearer' but rather to refer to two stable persons, herself and her mother. He suggested that she had two sets of homonyms: $I_E$ and $you_M$ referring to herself; $I_M$ and $you_E$ referring to her mother. (The subscripts (E) and (M) refer, respectively, to the use of these words in the speech of Eve and in the speech of her mother, or to Eve's production on the one hand and comprehension on the other.) McNeill concluded that eventually the 'fractionated' morphemes must merge into a single $I$ and a single $you$. According to him the basis for this merging would be the concept of 'self-reference.' But identifying $I$ as the self-referring expression biases the definition to production only, and leaves comprehension out of consideration. $I$ refers to the self from the speaker's point of view but not from the hearer's. In the framework presented here – the acquisition of deictic categories – the basis for the merger would be concepts of 'speaker reference' and 'addressee reference.'

The problem of sorting out conversational roles is not manifested only in difficulties with personal pronouns. Menn (1978) has provided us with a sensitive account of related phenomena. She begins with the observation that in stereotyped very early conversational exchanges, both parties are supposed to say the same thing: 'hi,' 'bye-bye.' After children have discovered that speakers are supposed more often to say different things, there may still be residual misapprehensions that lead, for example, to saying 'thank you' when giving something. Children may erroneously assume that *both* participants in a giving transaction say 'thank you' or that both say 'please.'

## Personal pronouns in relation to other aspects of grammar

Bloom (1970) and Huxley (1970) both observe, on the basis of separate sets of data, that children who use pronouns correctly are not necessarily more advanced in other aspects of their grammar. In fact, both of them, somewhat to their surprise, find the opposite to be true. Bloom's Eric rarely referred to himself by name. His use of *I* as an agent of events developed early as a variant of a pre-verbal particle, /ð/. Bloom's Kathryn and Gia did use their proper names to refer to themselves as agents of events. But whereas Kathryn's and Gia's early grammars provided for concatenation of words in several grammatical functions, Eric's grammar was restricted to a narrower set of invariant constructions such as 'more ___,' 'my___,' etc. In the terminology of Brown and Bloom, derived from Braine's concept of 'pivot words' with stable positions, Eric followed a pivotal strategy in learning syntax.

Huxley noted a similar pattern. Douglas had much more difficulty with pronouns in general than did Katriona. She seldom referred to herself by name; he did so consistently. But on other indices of linguistic development, Douglas was ahead of Katriona. Huxley mentions in particular the greater complexity of his noun phrases, and his mastery of auxiliary inversion in questions.

Bloom and Huxley offer strikingly different interpretations of these parallel sets of facts. Huxley entertains the possibility of a 'zero-sum' explanation. If children focus their energy on one aspect of their grammar, other developments will be neglected or even impeded.

It is possible that [Douglas'] greater difficulty over pronouns was due to the fact that his linguistic structure as a whole was more complex and that Katriona's, whose structures are generally easier, with fewer variables to manipulate [sic] . . . [This] leaves us with the predicament that early success in one part of the grammar might actually be interpreted as implying some impediment of progress in other parts. (Huxley, 1970: 159)

Huxley expresses the hope that this is not the case.

Bloom's interpretation may offer one way of avoiding this conclusion. She proposes that both Eric's superficially sophisticated use of *I* and his unsophisticated pivot-like sentence structure are due to a single strategy in language learning: the search for constant forms. Sentences beginning with *I* followed by a verb and ending with *it* represent such invariant forms, which Eric then adopted wholesale.

Katriona's speech is probably not susceptible to the same analysis. Her first-person subject forms are not invariant in that she alternates between *I, me, my* and *mys*. And her sentence forms (reported at a more advanced stage than Eric's) are also more variable.

Both Huxley's and Bloom's discussions raise the question of the degree of integration in children's progress in learning to speak their language. Are there necessary connections between their approach in one area (e.g. reference) and in another that is superficially unrelated (e.g. the expression of basic grammatical relations)? Huxley seems to assume that there must be integration, and therefore interprets the apparent discrepancies in her data as evidence of negative correlation. The assumption may not be warranted.

## Disturbances of the personal reference system in autism

Certain distortions in the use of personal pronouns have been observed to be associated with the psychopathological condition of childhood autism. A variety of syndromes have been described, including failure to use pronouns and using *I* for the addressee and *you* for the self (Rutter, Greenfield & Lockyer, 1968). In fact, these language disorders have come to be regarded as diagnostic of autism (Kanner, 1949).

From their psychiatric and psychoanalytic vantage points, the researchers who have focused on these syndromes have attributed them to 'loss of self' or failure to develop a stable concept of self. They treat confusion about *I* and *you* as a direct reflection of confusion about the boundaries between self and other.

However, this interpretation does not take into account the 'shifting' properties of the personal reference system, which may well be the key to the difficulties autistic children encounter when using it.[1] Bettelheim (1967) has dramatically documented the struggle of autistic children to achieve sameness and mechanical predictability in the environment. He considers this struggle to be the basis of their cognitive and social

---

[1] Since this was written, Lise Menn has brought to my attention a paper by Ricks & Wing (1975) which likewise interprets autistic children's difficulties with pronouns as arising from their 'shifting' properties. Ricks & Wing in turn cite Bartak, Rutter & Cox (1975) as their source for this idea.

orientation. It is possible that the same principle extends from their relations with objects to their handling of language. A simple and direct way to arrest the vicissitudes of *I* and *you* is to treat them as ordinary referential labels. Children are addressed as *you*; therefore they will refer to themselves as *you*. Their addressees refer to themselves as *I*; therefore children will call them *I*.

In the literature on autism the pattern is called 'pronominal reversal.' The name reflects the psychiatric interpretation of the phenomenon. Psychiatrists see it as talking in opposites. Bettelheim credits the child who does this with a certain intelligent perversity: 'Such talking in reverse, or in opposites, is not easy for a small child to do and further demonstrates his capacity for logic. It is not easy to talk consistently in opposites, to do quite well in getting across what is wanted, and never once make the "mistake" of using pronouns correctly' (Bettelheim, 1967: 243).

For this interpretation to make sense, children's language must be examined exclusively in terms of production, without taking into account the conversational situation as a whole. Children are supposed to say *I*, but say *you* instead, or they are supposed to say *you* and say *I* instead. Therefore, according to Bettelheim and others, they are speaking in opposites, or in a pattern of 'pronominal reversal.' In fact, the reverse is true. If the speech of autistic children is examined in the context of the general language input they receive and of the particular conversational situation, their problem is actually one of *failure* to reverse pronouns. They are addressed as *you* and therefore they call themselves *you*. The syndrome might more accurately be called 'pronominal nonreversal.'

The 'pronominal reversal' view uses evidence from children's language behavior without analyzing the structure of the language domain. In default of a grammatical analysis of person reference, these psychologists seem to assume that the analysis implicitly made by autistic children is the same as their own. They are then free to read the children's language deviations directly as psychological metaphor, much as one would read poetry.

To clarify the pattern of inference described and criticized above I would like to give another example of its application. Bettelheim observes that there is a delay in autistic children's use of *yes* as compared with their use of *no*. He cites this as evidence of their 'negativism.' This inference overlooks several important facts: that affirmation and negation aren't mirror operations in communication; that the lexical item *yes* does not play exactly the same role in affirming or agreeing as *no* does in denying or disagreeing; and that all children use *no* before they use *yes*. Again, a direct metaphorical reading is given to language behavior, without regard to the fact that the language fragments under consideration are part of a structure with systematic properties.

Returning to the 'pronominal nonreversal' view of autistic pronoun usage, it also casts a different light on the failure of certain children to use *I*. Bettelheim considers that the 'avoidance of I . . . [is] either a denial of selfhood, or denotes an absence of awareness of selfhood' (Bettelheim, 1967: 426). The alternative is that the children have coded *I* as the label for their addressees. The relative 'avoidance' of *I* in their speech would then correspond to the relative 'avoidance' of *you* by normal young children. Neither group refer to their addressees as often as they refer to themselves.

Bettelheim's notion that autistic children specifically avoid *I* seems to stem from observations about the nature of their repetitive speech as well as from the infrequency of *I* in their speech in general. Kanner (1949) noted that autistic children echo the speech of their addressees. The following is presented by Bettelheim as an example of such an interaction:

(17) Adult: Do you want milk?
     Child: You want milk.

Some researchers have suggested that the apparent 'pronominal reversal' of autistic children may result from 'echolalia.' Bettelheim disagrees. He points out that these children imitate selectively. They would not repeat, 'I want milk.' In the context of what is seen as a general imitative tendency, the failure to imitate *I* must be construed as motivated avoidance. Again, an alternative view, consistent with the 'pronominal nonreversal' interpretation is possible. In the example above, the child who says, 'You want milk' may not be imitating but may instead be replying affirmatively to a question about his desires and using *you* as the label for himself. He fails to repeat, 'I want milk,' because he understands it, correctly, as a statement about his interlocutor's wishes which demands no reply on his part.

The children who exhibit 'pronominal reversal' or, according to my interpretation, 'pronominal nonreversal,' at least have a systematic way of distinguishing between *I* and *you*, although their way does not correspond to that of the language. Other children seem to realize only that both terms refer in some fluctuating manner to participants in the conversational situation. They use one or both pronouns unsystematically or according to an idiosyncratic system that they have devised in order to stabilize the fluctuations. Bettelheim's case descriptions include children who use one of the pronouns for both self and addressee, and others who use both pronouns for self *or* addressee.

The proposal that errors in the use of pronouns made by autistic children are attributable to the 'shifting' properties of the pronouns rather than directly due to confusion about 'self' may be tested by examining their handling of proper names. If the source of their difficulty is confusion about the identity of self and other, then they should apply their names to other people and/or vice versa. If the source of their difficulty is the 'shifting' properties of personal pronouns, then they should use proper names correctly.

The 'pronominal nonreversal' interpretation of autistic pronoun usage is not actually an alternative explanation of the phenomenon or indeed an explanation at all. Rather it is an alternative way of construing what needs to be explained. It offers a reformulation of what autistic children are doing when they use *I* for *you* and *you* for *I*, or when they fail to use *I*, but it does not state why they continue to have difficulties that normal children outgrow or bypass completely. Perhaps the answer to this question will be stated once again in terms of their confusion about 'self' and 'other', as it was in the 'pronominal reversal' view. But the explanation will have an extra step that takes into account the properties of the medium in which the symptom is expressed.

Whatever psychological explanation is found for the language disorder, it will be pertinent to an understanding of the normal development of person reference. A particular explanation of an abnormal or unusual case commits us to a particular explanation of the normal. Since formulations of normal language development at the present time do not incorporate many specifically psychological terms, the psychological explanation of 'pronominal nonreversal' will be an isolated fragment waiting to be incorporated in a psychological theory of language development and thus partially specifying the form of such a theory.

## A study of pronoun alternation in discourse

In question and answer discourse, first- and second-person elements alternate systematically. Katz & Postal (1964:114) call this a 'curious but universal fact.' Jespersen (1965) remarks on more elaborate and variable patterns of alternation in reported speech. These involve rotation between first-, second- and third-person elements. The experiments to be reported here tested children's ability to handle these patterns of alternation. The experiments employed a combination of question–answer discourse and indirect speech.

## Procedure

The basic format was to ask the child to ask someone else particular questions. The questions all involved pronominal reference to at least one of the three participants in discourse. In a pilot study, the experimenter, the subject, and the question recipient were all seated together in one room. This situation was quite artificial, since the question recipient could hear each question before the child asked it. It seemed that children might have objections to carrying out so redundant a task. And even if they didn't, their performance might be detrimentally affected. So, in the main study, the experimenter and the question recipient were seated in different rooms, and the child had to carry the questions across some distance from one to the other. This situation has a different disadvantage in that it puts a greater burden on the children's memory. In both conditions the question recipient gave an answer to each question asked by the child.

The subjects' questions were taped and transcribed.

## Materials

Some examples of the instructions are:

(18) Category 1. Ask Tom if I have blue eyes.
     Category 2. Ask Tom where you should sit.
     Category 3. Ask Tom if he is tired.

(The category number corresponds to the person in the instructions.)
     The relaying or reporting of these questions requires a change in the pronouns. The child should ask:

(19) 1'. Does she have blue eyes?
     2'. Where should I sit?
     3'. Are you tired?

In this particular discourse situation the pronominal rotation is always as follows:

(20)  1″. first person→third person
        2″. second person→first person
        3″. third person→second person

In the second experiment another type of question was also included. The subject was a fourth party, usually a teacher, identified by name.

(21)  4. Ask Tom where Kathy lives.

Here the third-person subject remains in the third person when the question is relayed:

(22)  4′. Where does Kathy live?

The questions included both *yes/no*-questions and *wh*-questions. The pronouns included nominative, genitive, accusative, and dative forms. Sometimes more than one deictic pronoun was included in the same sentence. (For a full listing of the questions see appendixes B and C.)

### Subjects

In the pilot study the subjects were twenty-six children from the University of Chicago Nursery School. They ranged in age from 3;6 to 5;1.

In the main study the subjects were twenty-two children from the Toddlers' Campus Nursery School in Champaign, ranging in age from 2;7 to 5;3.

## Results and discussion
### Pilot study: all participants seated together

The overall rate of error was low. It was 9 per cent in categories 1 and 2, and there were no errors in category 3 (see table 7). Furthermore errors were widely scattered across subjects. No children were consistent in making errors. They were usually correct and only made an occasional error here and there.

There was consistency, however, in the types of errors. Eleven of twelve errors in category 1 involved use of the second person in the question. For example, the experimenter said to the child:

(23) Ask Tom where my bicycle is.

The child asked Tom:

(24) Where is your bicycle?

All seven errors in category 2 involved use of the second person. The experimenter said:

(25) Ask Tom what your middle name is.

The child asked Tom:

(26) What's your middle name?

One conceivable source of errors might have been the children's interpretation of the experimenter's directions as containing a direct quotation of a question rather than a subordinated question. If the children did not attend to cues of noninversion of subject and verb and lack of question intonation, or if they did not 'read' them correctly,

TABLE 7. *Pronouns. Type of errors on* I/you/he *question task* (*pilot study*)

|  | Category 1 | Category 2 | Category 3 |
|---|---|---|---|
| Person in experimenter's instructions | 1 | 2 | 3 |
| Person required in subject's relayed question | 3 | 1 | 2 |
| Type of error: (Actual person in subject's relayed question) |  |  |  |
| 1 | 1 | doesn't apply | 0 |
| 2 | 11 | 7 | doesn't apply |
| 3 | doesn't apply | 0 | 0 |
| Total number of errors | 12 (9%) | 7 (9%) | 0 |
| Number of subjects making errors[a] | 8 (31%) | 5 (19%) | 0 |

[a] n = 26.

then they might have registered the experimenter's directions alternatively as (27) or (28):

(27) Ask Tom where you should sit.
(28) Ask Tom, 'where you should sit?'

Since children in this age range do not always apply subject/verb inversion in questions, the second reading may be possible for them. If a child did adopt this interpretation, then a response like (29),

(29) Where you should sit?

with failure to shift, would not be incorrect.

But the hypothesis that errors are due to confusion between quoted and subordinated questions lacks generality. It can account only for the errors in a single category, category 2, where all the errors consisted of retaining the second-person pronoun instead of shifting from second to first. The hypothesis predicts other errors of failure to shift, but there were no errors in category 3, and only one of twelve errors in category 1 was a failure to shift.

The other eleven errors in category 1 consisted of pronoun shifts, but incorrect ones. The children carried out instructions like (30),

(30) Ask Tom if I could sing.

with a question like (31),

(31) (To Tom): Can you sing?

This type of error may reflect overlearning of the typical pattern of alternation that occurs in two-person discourse when the two participants take turns responding to each other. In that situation, *I* and *you* alternate symmetrically. For each participant, heard *I* refers to the same person as spoken *you*; heard *you* refers to the same person as spoken *I*. In the three-participant situation part of this pattern, but not all of it, changes. For children relaying questions, heard *you* still referred to spoken *I*, but heard *I* had now to become spoken *he/she*. Perhaps the children who made errors were assimilating three-party discourse to the pattern of two-party discourse.[1]

[1] Rips (personal communication) has pointed out to me that this interpretation leads to the expectation that category 2 (in which the experimenter's instructions applied to the second person, and the subject's response should have been first person) would be easy. The fact that it was not, makes the interpretation questionable.

One child (age 5) recognized her difficulty in relaying the first-person instructions in a very striking way. In each occurrence of a category 1 item (shifting from first to third person), and only in their occurrence, she demurred, saying that she did not know how to do it. Scattered through her protocols are exchanges like this:

(32) Experimenter: Ask Tom where I live.
Beth: . . . *that* would be *hard* for me.

(33) Experimenter: Ask Tom what my favorite color is.
Beth: That would be hard too.

(34) Experimenter: Ask Tom what I said on the telephone.
Beth: What did you say . . . well I don't think I can do that.

Two interpretations of the children's errors have been offered. Each one is limited in application to errors in a single category of items. But the errors in both categories have one important common feature: the second person, *you*, is made the subject of the question. The only category where no errors occurred is the one where *you* is *supposed* to be made the subject of the question. Perhaps then what the errors reveal is a pragmatic tendency to address questions about someone to that person, and, conversely, to turn questions addressed to someone into questions about that person.

Because the rate of error was so low, I thought errors might be eliminated altogether by changing the situation to make it less artificial. The artificiality of asking the children to ask questions of a third party who was present, and could hear the question before being asked it, may have created confusion about precisely those deictic coordinates of discourse that were being tested.

### Final study: experimenter and question recipient in different rooms

Despite the fact that the subjects in this second version of the experiment included much younger children (beginning age 2;7), the rate of error was lower than in the pilot study (beginning age 3;6). But errors were not eliminated completely.

For instructions with the first, second, and third person, the rate of error was respectively 5 per cent, 7 per cent, and 3 per cent (see table 8). The errors were scattered fairly uniformly across the subjects. No individual child made more than two errors. (This generalization must be qualified, however, because some of the youngest children only

TABLE 8. *Pronouns. Type of errors on* I/you/he *question task* (*final study*)

| | Category 1 | Category 2 | Category 3 | |
|---|---|---|---|---|
| Person in experimenter's instructions | 1 | 2 | 3-Pro | 3-Noun |
| Person required in subject's relayed question | 3 | 1 | 2 | 3-Noun |
| Type of error: (Actual person in subject's relayed question) | | | | |
| 1 | 1 | doesn't apply | 0 | 0 |
| 2 | 5 | 7 | doesn't apply | 0 |
| 3 | doesn't apply | 0 | 2 | 0 |
| Total | 6 | 7 | 2 | 0 |
| Errors as percentage of recorded responses | 5 | 7 | 3 | 0 |
| Number of subjects making errors[a] | 5 (23%) | 6 (27%) | 2 (9%) | 0 |

[a] $n = 22$.

carried out a few of the instructions. For them one or two errors constitute a higher proportion of responses.) None of the five oldest children (4;9 and above) made any errors involving person.

It was difficult to get the younger subjects to persevere in the task and several of their protocols are therefore incomplete. Data for different categories of items show different degrees of incompleteness. To try to compensate for this, the percentage of errors (in table 8) is calculated not in relation to the number of items in the complete test but in relation to the number of responses actually recorded.

The types of errors were distributed similarly to those in the pilot study. There were more errors in categories 1 and 2 than in category 3. It is apparently easiest for children to follow instructions to ask a person a question about that person himself.

In category 1 items, the experimenter instructed the children to ask a question about herself (the experimenter). In relaying the question, they should have converted the subject from first person to third. Out of a total of six errors, five consisted of second-person questions. For example:

(35) Experimenter: Ask Tom where my bicycle is.
     Subject (to Tom): Where is your bicycle is?

One consisted of a first-person question:

(36) Experimenter: Ask Tom what I found yesterday.
     Subject (to Tom): What did I found?

In category 2 items, the experimenter instructed the children to ask about themselves. The children should have converted the second-person instructions to a first-person question. All seven errors consisted of second-person questions. Two errors occurred as unique errors on two different test items. One is as follows:

(37) Experimenter: Ask Tom to guess what your middle name is.
     Subject (to Tom): What's your middle name?

But the five others clustered together on a single item:

(38) Experimenter: Ask Tom where you should put this.
     Subject (to Tom): Where could you put this?

The clustering suggests that they may not be errors after all, but reflections of a different interpretation of the *you* in the instructions. The five children who made these 'errors' probably understood *you* not as the definite second-person pronoun, but rather as the indefinite *one*, as in 'Ask Tom where one should put this.' If so, then their retention of *you* in the actual question is correct. In deontological expressions, i.e. expressions about obligation which pertain to 'what you should do,' *you* is particularly susceptible to interpretation as *one*. On two occasions the question recipient prompted the children by repeating the instructions with contrastive stress on the *you*: 'No, ask where *you* should put it.' The stressed pronoun has only a second-person reading. In both cases, the children rephrased the question in the first person: 'Where should I put it?' Under this interpretation, the number of errors in category 2 is reduced to two.

In category 3 items, the experimenter instructed children to ask about the third party. The children should have converted the third-person instructions to a second-person question. Both of the errors in this category consisted of retaining the third person. For example:

(39) Experimenter: Ask Dick if he's tired.
    Subject (to Dick): He tired?                                    (No. 29)

Relaying questions vs. answering them

Some children sometimes provided an answer to the question instead of asking it. This occurred a total of twenty-four times. Twenty of these times were when the instructions were for the children to ask a question about themselves. C. Chomsky (1969) has documented children's problems in discriminating *ask* and *tell*. In the present experiment a number of children interpreted *ask* as either *ask* or *tell* according to pragmatic considerations. If they didn't know the answer they asked the question. If they did know the answer or if they had a stake in a particular answer, they showed a tendency to provide it. This suggests that children who 'tell' when requested to 'ask,' may not have a problem with the lexical meaning of *ask* after all. Instead of interpreting instructions to ask someone something as a request to demonstrate linguistic knowledge, they may be interpreting them as a request for information. In that case, supplying the information is an entirely appropriate response. The following example illustrates this principle of ordinary discourse:

(40) Tom: Ask Craig what he's bringing to the picnic.
    Jerry: Eggplant Istanbul. (I talked to him this morning.)

Only one child, the youngest (age 2;7), consistently gave answers that he obviously must have invented rather than ask the questions. For example:

(41) Experimenter: Ask Judy what I found.
    Subject (to Judy): She found these.

In fact he had no way of knowing what the experimenter had found. Out of eight responses made by this boy, four were of this type. In this case, it is dubious whether he knew the lexical meaning of *ask*.

Even when children supplied an answer (to the experimenter) instead of asking a question (of the recipient) it was usually possible to score their response for pronoun shifting. As it happens, the circumstance in which answers were most often supplied is also the one in which the pronoun shift is the same whether the child relays the question or answers it.

(42) Experimenter: Ask Tom if you've been good.
Subject (to experimenter): I've been good.

or,

Subject (to Tom): Have I been good?

The correct pronoun for the child to use in either case is *I*. This identity applies only for instructions with a second-person pronoun. It doesn't hold for instructions to ask questions about the speaker or the third party.

## General applicability of the message-relaying technique

In general, the technique of having children deliver messages or questions seems to be a potentially useful experimental device for language acquisition research. Many children were enthusiastic about carrying out this mission. The method lends itself to the investigation of syntactic and possibly also pragmatic questions. In this study, for example, many interesting patterns of question formation emerged. Some examples of common errors are as follows:

(43) a. Is Kathy's eyes blue?    Number agreement
 b. Is Kathy's eyes are blue?    Duplication of verb
     (*yes*/*no*-question)
 c. What did she found?    Tense duplication
 d. Where is her bicycle is?    Duplication of verb
     (*wh*-question)
 e. Did I be good?    Incorrect auxiliary
 f. What do you don't like to eat?    Double *do*-support in
     negative questions

# 5 *Demonstratives and deictic locatives*

## Introduction

Utterances are 'situated' in multiple layers of context. Some of these are as rich and abstract as the culture of the participants, or as their role relations. But the most concrete and basic way that utterances are situated is that they take place in some physical location. The speaker and addressee are in a spatial relation to each other, to the site(s) of their conversation, to the items discussed. Many languages incorporate devices that specifically link the utterance with its spatial context.

English does so with the demonstratives *this* and *that* and the spatial adverbs *here* and *there*. The terms in each pair contrast along a dimension of proximity to the speaker. Some languages mark this dimension in an obligatory fashion. Somali (Cassirer, 1953), for example, possesses three forms of the article, differing from each other in the final vowel. The article ending in -*a* is used in designating a thing or person in immediate proximity to the speaker and visible to him. The article ending in -*o* indicates a person or thing somewhat removed from the speaker, but still visible to him. The article ending in -*i* is used in referring to someone or something not visible to the speaker. In English the marking is optional. Although *this* and *that* can be used as articles as well as pronouns, there is also the option of using the spatially neutral *the*. The two dimensions, proximity–distance and visibility–invisibility, correlate loosely. Things that are nearby are more likely to be visible than distant objects. Some languages mark exclusively this second variable. Malagasy has particles indicating whether an object is visible to the speaker or not (Keenan, 1971). (Perhaps this constellation should also include the epistemological markers, compulsory in some languages, that indicate whether something is known directly or by hearsay. Marking of directness of knowledge corresponds, on the propositional level, to marking of visibility on the level of nouns.)

The visible–invisible contrast is structured in a simpler way than the proximal–distal one. It is absolute and dichotomous: an object is either visible or not visible. But one cannot determine absolutely whether an object is proximate or distant. Like terms of size such as *big*, adjectives of distance are inherently relative. A description of an object as *big* requires for its interpretation some assessment of typical size for its class. A *big mouse* is big relative to other mice. A description that implies or states that an object is proximate or distant requires the application of a scale of distance that is implicit in the discourse context, but not overtly stated.

## The meaning of *this* and *that* and *here* and *there*

Definitions of the deictic terms of location are more complex than definitions of the deictic pronouns. Questions of boundaries that do not exist in the latter domain arise in the former, and cannot be answered except by recourse to pragmatic considerations.

Lyons (1968: 275) defines *here* and *there* parenthetically as 'in the vicinity of the speaker: not in the vicinity of the speaker.' Fillmore (1971d: 5) defines *here* derivatively, on the basis of *this*. '*Here*, when used for locating objects, is paraphrasable as *in this place*.' And *this*, in turn, 'followed by the appropriate noun, locates an object as being in the same area as the speaker is at coding time.' In his subtle discussion of deictic phenomena he omits basic definitions of *that* and *there*. The reader 'knows' of course what they mean, and pinning that meaning down precisely is difficult. It certainly isn't absolutely true that *there* must mean 'not in the vicinity of the speaker.' Consider such examples as (1):

(1) A (rubbing B's stiff shoulder): Where does it hurt?
    B: Right there.

*There* can probably be used to point to any part of one's own body, except perhaps to a location right behind the eyes, the site of the homunculus who directs one's activities. The example above is offered not merely as a quibble but to suggest the vagaries that children are faced with as they learn how the system works.

In general, *here* means in the same location as the speaker, but the scope of *here* is, as Fillmore says, 'as general, or as vague, as the scope of the noun *place* ... *Here* [can] mean anything from "at this point"

[to] "in this galaxy."' The position of the addressee may be included in the speaker's *here*, or excluded, in which case the addressee is *there*. The distinction bears some resemblance to that between inclusive and exclusive *we* where the addressee himself is either included or excluded in the first-person pronoun. *There* is some other place, which may be near the speaker or far from the speaker in absolute terms, but which is being treated in some sense as not the location of the speaker.

R. Lakoff (1974: XVII-2-4) says that 'an object is identified by the use of *this* as being near at hand, usually near to the speaker rather than the addressee if there is a distinction ... *That* is used of an object far from the speaker, particularly when contrasted with another, closer.' Again, this can be considered a distillation of what the mature speaker knows about *this* and *that*. Children, who have the task of arriving at this distillation, will on many occasions encounter *that* used by a speaker to talk about something near at hand. The most telling examples, again, are ones in which the speaker is talking about his own body, presumably near him at all times:

(2) And that scar is from when the rope broke during a fire drill in college.

The situations in which the *this/that* and *here/there* contrasts emerge most clearly are those in which both terms of a pair are actually used contrastively and with contrastive stress. The fact that normal conversation frequently makes the contrasts explicit by means of negative or disjunctive sentences such as (3) and (4) may facilitate children's discovery of them.

(3) Not there. Over here.
(4) Do you want this one or that one?

Many other contrasts that are notorious for the difficulty children have with them (e.g. *more* vs. *less*) are seldom identified explicitly as contrasting terms in ordinary conversation. In other words, they are not typically used simultaneously to express a contrast.

Extensions of the deictic terms

Fillmore has pointed out that the spatial deictic terms can be used in three ways, varying according to the nature of the information that actually identifies the location. He calls these ways *gestural*, *symbolic*, and *anaphoric*, and offers the following examples:

(5) I want you to put it there.

(6) (On the telephone) Is Johnny there?

(7) I drove the car to the parking lot and left it there.

An accompanying physical gesture is required to identify where *there* is in (5). In (6) the general formula applies: *there* is 'the place where you are.' In (7) *there* is a place that has been identified in earlier discourse. Strictly speaking this final use is not deictic.

R. Lakoff (1974) offers a different trichotomy of deictic expressions in her discussion of *this* and *that*: *spatio-temporal deixis*, *discourse deixis*, and *emotional deixis*. The spatio-temporal category seems to subsume Fillmore's gestural and symbolic categories. It has to do with the indication of real space–time coordinates and it does not depend on discourse to be interpretable. Lakoff calls this the 'basic' demonstrative. The discourse category is close to Fillmore's anaphoric category with perhaps one difference. Lakoff, like Fillmore, talks about the use of *this* and *that* to refer to an object mentioned in prior discourse as in (8).

(8) I saw Fred in his new sombrero. $\left\{ \begin{array}{c} \text{This} \\ \text{That} \end{array} \right\}$ hat is really some-

thing.                                               (Lakoff, 1974: XXIII-2)

But under the same rubric she also talks about the use of demonstratives to refer to prior (or subsequent) discourse itself, as in (9).

(9) Now this is what we must do: round up all the usual suspects . . .
                                               (Lakoff, 1974: XXVII-2)

The proximal–distal contrast of spatio-temporal demonstratives has some manifestations in discourse deixis. For example, *this* can be used only when its antecedent remark was uttered by the same speaker, as in (10a) and not when it was uttered by a different speaker, as in (10b). Borrowing an illustration from Lakoff again:

(10) Speaker: Dick says that the Republicans may have credibility problems.

    a. Same speaker continuing: $\left\{ \begin{array}{c} \text{This} \\ \text{That} \end{array} \right\}$ is an understatement.

or

    b. Different speaker: $\left\{ \begin{array}{c} \text{*This} \\ \text{That} \end{array} \right\}$ is an understatement.

In other words, *this* is restricted to comments on remarks that are 'close to the speaker' in the sense that they were made by him.

Only *this* can be used in 'forward anaphora' (henceforth, 'cataphora') (see (11a)).

(11) a. What I know for sure is $\left\{ \begin{array}{l} \text{this} \\ \text{*that} \end{array} \right\}$ : beef prices are going up.

    b. Beef prices are going up: $\left\{ \begin{array}{l} \text{this} \\ \text{that} \end{array} \right\}$ I know for sure.

By contrast either *this* or *that* can be used in anaphora (see (11b)).

The two restrictions demonstrated in (10) and (11) are complementary. They converge in the effect of linking anaphoric *this* with the speech of the speaker. The first states that speakers can use *this* in discourse anaphora only when referring back to their *own* speech. The second states that *this* is the only form of the demonstrative which can be employed in cataphora. Since in unplanned discourse speakers can make specific reference only to their own future statements (not knowing the future statements of others), *this* remains tied to the speaker's own remarks.

Lakoff's third category is emotional deixis under which she places 'a host of problematical uses, generally linked to the speaker's emotional involvement in the subject-matter of his utterance' (p. xvii-3). She points out the curious fact that in this category both forms of the demonstrative, the proximal *this*, and the distal *that* can be used to achieve 'closeness,' as in her examples in (12) and (13):

(12) This Henry Kissinger is really something!
(13) How's that throat?

The preceding discussion demonstrates that the ramifications of the *this/that* and *here/there* distinctions are complex, extending from deixis to anaphora and discourse anaphora, from spatial proximity and distance to various metaphorical extensions of proximity and distance.

### Distance as a subsidiary meaning

Although the distinction between *this* and *that* and between *here* and *there* is a distinction between the proximal and the distal, the terms themselves do not refer to the dimension of distance in the same way that *near* and *far* do. They will not serve, for example, to answer directly the question, 'How far is it?' Prototypic answers to that question would be stated in terms of a description of the distance, perhaps quantitative (e.g. 'two miles'), perhaps not (e.g. 'on the same block'), or as a subjective judgment (e.g. 'not too far'). What *here* and *there* can answer directly are questions about location. What *this* and *that* can answer directly are questions about identity. The proximal–distal contrast between the terms in each pair is not their primary sense, but rather a subsidiary aspect of meaning, subordinate to location and identification, respectively.

It would seem then that children must have a special problem discovering the basic fact that the dimension of distance underlies the contrast between the deictic spatial terms. The nondeictic spatial terms, those relating to distance and those relating to other spatial parameters as well, are used when the dimensions they encode are a topic of conversation. The fact that the words *tall* and *short* are used when people are talking about height will help children to map them onto this dimension. More inference is required to map *here* and *there* and *this* and *that* onto the dimension of distance. There is, however, a type of usage which probably facilitates the mapping. Sometimes both terms are used contrastively in one expression, as in (14) and (15), and accompanied by pointing:

(14) Do you want this one or that one?
(15) Don't put it over here; put it over there.

## Point of reference

When language is used that actually *measures* distance, it is possible (though not necessary) to state a point of reference.

(16) Saigon is 700 miles from Hanoi.

The same possibility exists in expressions that don't actually measure distance but that are used to talk explicitly about relative proximity and distance.

(17) Saigon is far away from Hanoi.

The deictic terms *this* and *that* and *here* and *there* are used without stating the point of reference. It remains implicit, and is always the speaker.

The nondeictic terms of distance also can be used without overt statement of the point of reference.

(18) San Jose isn't far.

The analysis has been proposed (H. Clark, 1973: 44) that here too the unstated point of reference is the location of the speaker. But in fact it is not limited to the speaker. The sentence above could appropriately be uttered by a person in Chicago speaking on the telephone to a friend in San Francisco who is complaining about a trip he has to make to San Jose. In that case the unstated point of reference is the location of the hearer. In other contexts it could equally be the location of any discourse topic, as Fillmore has also pointed out.

The fact that the point of reference for the deictic expressions of proximity and distance is always the speaker has an important corollary; the point of reference shifts back and forth as the speakers take turns in a conversation. Once it is discovered, this pattern is clear, stable, and invariant. Before it is discovered, it may be a source of great confusion, since it allows the location 'here' to be in any number of places at once.

By contrast, the point of reference of the nondeictic expressions remains constant. This is obviously so when the point of reference is mentioned. Less obviously, it is also the case when the point of reference is unstated. Returning to the phone conversation between San Francisco and Chicago:

(19) Speaker (Chicago): San Jose isn't far.
    Speaker (San Francisco): Yes it is.
    Speaker (Chicago):  a.  *It's not even as far as Champaign.
                     b.  It's not even as far as Champaign is

$$\text{from} \left\{ \begin{array}{l} \text{here.} \\ \text{Chicago.} \end{array} \right\}$$

The unacceptability of (19a) shows that when the point of reference has been San Francisco, a change in the point of reference must be explicitly signaled in some way. The speaker in Chicago can't suddenly start using his own location as a point of reference without indicating that he is doing so.

## Proximity as an elementary spatial relationship

Although, as the preceding section demonstrated, the ramifications of the contrast between *this* and *that* and *here* and *there* are complex, the core of the contrast taps a very primitive principle of cognitive organization: proximity.

According to Piaget (1967a: 6) proximity is

the most elementary spatial relationship which can be grasped by perception . . . corresponding to the simplest type of perceptual structurization, namely, the 'nearbyness' of elements belonging to the same perceptual field . . . Following the work of the Gestalt School, it is well known that the primary factor in the organization of structures is undoubtedly the proximity of structural elements . . . The younger the child, the greater the importance of proximity as compared with other factors of organization (resemblance, symmetry, etc.).

Piaget elaborates these ideas into the general thesis that topological space is primary and Euclidean space a late achievement in the child's cognitive development.

Piaget's discussion applies to children's perception of spatial relationships between two objects. Probably the same claim can be extended to their perception of spatial relationships between themselves and other objects. Proximity is the most basic of these relationships. Apparently proximity to self is represented even at the neuronal level. Mountcastle (1975) reports that the 'visual fixation neurons' of the cortex of the inferior parietal lobule of the monkey discharge with greater frequency as a function of the proximity of the object the animal fixates on. The discharge rate is highest when the object is within reach.

It is important to note that Piaget does not say that the dimension proximity–distance is elementary for children. Instead it is the pole of proximity that is basic. The elaboration of the bipolar dimension requires further cognitive development. As perception becomes more 'analytic,' children can 'take account of different degrees of "proximity" operating over larger areas, instead of being confined to the relation of immediate proximity' (p. 7). Presumably the perception of diminishing degrees of proximity shades off eventually into a concept of the negation of proximity, or distance.

By the time children are learning to talk, the rudiments of the proximity–distance dimension have been consolidated. Piaget (1954) describes this degree of elaboration of the spatial field as an achievement of the sensory-motor period. But even under the assumption that both poles of the dimension are available to children conceptually, it can be argued that it will be easier for them to learn the meanings of words that

map onto the concept of proximity. The same perceptual factors that
made proximity the most elementary spatial relationship will, in a
separate line of influence, make the terminology of proximity easier
to grasp than the terminology of distance.

Let us consider a caricature of the situation children are confronted
with. They are surrounded by objects and people. The people engage
in activities with the objects, with each other, and with the children.
Sometimes they talk. In the course of events they will mention that *X is
near* (or *close to*) *Y*, or that *X is far away from Y*. Assuming that the
children know what X and Y refer to, but do not know the meanings of
the relational terms, how do they discover their meanings? The communication has suggested that some relationship exists between X and
Y. If X and Y are near each other, then their spatial relationship in at
least some contexts is immediately salient. If they are far away from
each other then other possible relationships, such as similarity in
various attributes, are foregrounded at the expense of the spatial relationship which is relatively weak. *Near* (or *close*) can signal a readily
perceptible spatial relation. *Far* signals a relation that is more likely to
be imperceptible. Thus, it would seem easier for children to discover
that *near* (or *close*) has to do with relations in space and with proximity
than to discover that *far* has to do with relations in space and with
distance.

Similarly for the deictic terms. The demonstrative *this* applies to
something which is present. *Here* applies to a location which is in some
sense 'present.'[1] By contrast, things that can be referred to as *that*
or *that N*, and locations that can be referred to as *there* are not necessarily
present in the context. Therefore the nature of the relationship signalled
by *this* and *here* will be relatively more accessible to the child.

## Predictions from H. Clark's marking hypothesis

In his model for the acquisition of spatial and temporal terms, H.
Clark (1973) offers the generalization that unmarked terms will be
acquired before marked terms. For the domain of distance, he identifies
*far*, *there*, and *that* as the unmarked members of their respective pairs.

---

[1] If the scale of the discourse topic gets very large, as in 'here on earth' or even 'here
in Champaign,' the sense in which the location is present will no longer facilitate the
child's decoding of the proximal sense of the term. 'Earth' and 'Champaign' are not
present in easily perceptible ways. The facilitating contexts are those in which *this*
or *here* can be indicated concretely and unambiguously.

Therefore, the prediction follows that *far*, *there*, and *that*, will be learned earlier. I will first discuss the linguistic analysis, and then the rationale of the predictions that are based on it.

Using Bierwisch's (1967) test for markedness that asks which member of a contrasting pair of words can be used with fewer restricting conditions, *far* does emerge clearly as the unmarked member of the *far/near* (*close*) pairs. Sentence (20a) is easily understood; (20b) is not.

(20) a.  The lake is twice as far as the river.
     b.  ?The river is twice as close as the lake.

*Far* is also the term which applies in neutral questions:

(21) a.  How far is the lake?
     b.  How $\left\{ \begin{array}{c} \text{close} \\ \text{near} \end{array} \right\}$ is the lake?

Question (21b), pronounced with normal question intonation, pre-supposes that the lake is nearby. (There are ways of saying it, however, that indicate the speaker considers the lake to be far away. Imagine how a person might say it who wants to spend the day at the river but is told that the river is too far away and that he should go to the lake instead.) Question (21a) does not contain any presupposition with respect to distance.

However, *far* lacks another of the neutral uses frequently (though not always) attached to unmarked spatial adjectives. Namely, it cannot be used in measuring expressions:

(22) a.  It's forty miles long.
     b.  *It's one mile far.

Thus, *far* does not have as many neutral uses as, for example, *long*, but it is still unambiguously the unmarked member of the *far/close* pair.

Among the dimensional adjectives, *big/little*, *tall/short*, etc., the un-marked term also names the extended end of the dimension. *Far* follows this pattern too. It is the unmarked term and indicates the ex-tended end of the distance dimension. *There* and *that* are the extended terms of their respective pairs, and Clark reasons that they too should be unmarked. He argues that *there* is, in fact, unmarked on the basis of its use in sentences like (23):

(23) a.  There are three men there in the room.
     b.  There are three men here in the room.

Clark calls the initial existential *there* in these examples a 'neutral specification of location' (p. 48). This analysis has some appeal. At the very least the example establishes that *here*, which has no equivalent use, is not the more general term. But it is not completely clear that the existential *there* specifies location at all. A sentence like (24) focuses the question more sharply.

(24) There is no such thing as a hippoposthumous.

Here any residual locative meaning of *there* seems to have been erased.

In questions, the neutral specifier of location that operates most nearly like *how far* and *how long* is simply *where*. The spatial term is incorporated into the question word. Therefore, the form of neutral questions does not help to identify either *here* or *there* as unmarked.

Clark draws on Kuroda (1968) for the argument that *that* is the unmarked member of the *this/that* pair. Kuroda cites examples (25) and (26) as cases where *that* is used in a neutral way with respect to the *this/that* opposition:

(25) I know that.
(26) Let his fate and that of his poor wife be remembered.

The neutrality of (25) is contestable. The sentence involves a case of anaphora in which *that* refers to some prior discourse. If the reference were to subsequent discourse, as R. Lakoff (1974) has shown, the appropriate pronoun would be *this* as in (27).

(27) I know *this*: when the tough get going, the going gets tough.

Cataphora is relatively unusual, and unlike anaphora, is restricted to single-speaker discourse sequences. Therefore, the use of *this* is more specialized than the use of *that*. But it remains that *that* is not completely neutral.

Turning again to the question test, let us compare sentences (28) and (29):

(28) What's that?
(29) What's this?

Question (28) is the more general question, but it does not have absolute generality. If the speaker is holding the relevant object in his hand and examining it, only the question 'What's this?' is appropriate. Admittedly this is a special case, but the point is precisely that special cases exist.

By contrast, no distance between two points is so small that it makes the question 'How far apart are they?' inappropriate. These examples illustrate the difference between generality and neutrality. *Far* is truly neutral; *that* is merely general.

It turns out to be difficult to extrapolate the concept of markedness from the domain of spatial adjectives to the domain of deictic spatial terms. Using a weak criterion of unmarked as 'more general,' *there* and *that* do appear to be the unmarked terms. Using the strong criterion of unmarked as 'neutral,' it is questionable whether any of the terms are unmarked.

### Lyons' feature analysis

Lyons (1975) also analyzes *this* and *here* as marked in relation to *that* and *there*. His analysis, unlike Clark's, is based on overtly semantic criteria. Although Lyons and Clark both frame their analyses in terms of semantic features and agree that *this* and *here* are marked, their feature analyses are very different. H. Clark's and E. Clark's psycholinguistic predictions depend crucially on certain properties of their feature description that are not matched by Lyons.

E. Clark (1971) focuses on relations of super- and subordination between features. She represents the claim that a feature is superordinate by placing it higher in a feature list. And she argues that children learn components of word meaning by proceeding through feature lists from top to bottom.

H. Clark (1974) focuses on patterns of polarity in feature lists. Components of meaning that are 'conceptually positive' are considered to have a positive value on the appropriate semantic feature. Components of meaning that are 'conceptually negative' are treated as having a negative feature value. The presence of negation adds an increment of psychological complexity. All other things being equal, a word with more negative features will be harder for adults to process and for children to learn.

Lyons proposes the feature analysis of the spatial deictic terms shown overleaf. Point by point this analysis contradicts that of H. Clark. Whereas in the Clark analysis distance is superordinate to proximity, in the Lyons analysis proximity is superordinate to distance. Whereas in the Clark analysis the proximal terms have more negative features than the distal terms, in the Lyons analysis the distal terms have more negative

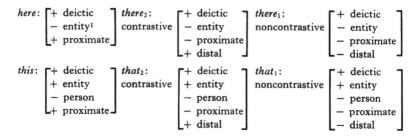

features than the proximal. Finally, in the Clark analysis the contrastive distal terms are treated as having one more negative feature than the non-contrastive distal terms. But in the Lyons analysis, the reverse is true.

Reiterating E. Clark and H. Clark's theoretical predictions, super-ordinate features will be acquired before subordinate features, and terms with fewer negative values on features will be learned before those with more. Applying these predictions to Lyons' feature analysis, one arrives at the following order of acquisition: *here* before contrastive *there* before noncontrastive *there*, and *this* before contrastive *that* before non-contrastive *that*. This is the exact reverse of the prediction that Clark and Clark make using their feature analysis. If this order were confirmed empirically, what would the implications be for their formulations? Would their theory be falsified, or would their feature analysis?

Of course Lyons did not have the same psycholinguistic model in mind when he formulated his feature description. In fact Lyons' description is formulated without a strong link between the formalism of bipolar features and any psycholinguistic theory. Accordingly, the point of this discussion is not to pit one prediction against another, or even one feature description against another, but to illustrate the fact that a common commitment to description in terms of semantic features does not necessarily yield identical or even compatible analyses of meaning.

Apparently there is no agreed upon algorithm for describing the meanings of words in terms of semantic features. E. Clark and H. Clark's semantic feature descriptions are not independent of their psycho-linguistic theory. The proposition that terms with extra negative features take longer to process cannot be confirmed unless there are independent means for evaluating which terms have extra negative features.

---

[1] Lyons admits that his choice of [− entity] rather than [+ locative] might be 'unsatisfactory.' It does seem so.

# A study of children's comprehension of the proximal–distal contrast in *this/that*, *here/there* and *close/far*

## Procedure

The subject and the experimenter were seated on the floor facing each other. The experimenter showed the subject two small plates, turned them upside down and said, 'I'm going to hide a penny under one of these plates, and you're supposed to guess where it is. Close your eyes and I'll hide it.' Later the child opened his eyes, guessed, and lifted the plate of his choice to find out if he was right. After two undirected guesses, two dolls representing small boys were brought out. 'Now these two boys are going to help you find it by telling you where to look.' The convention was established that when a doll was 'speaking' it would also be made to move, so that all concerned would know who was speaking. 'When they're talking, they'll go like this' – the first doll was agitated: 'Hello, my name is Billy.' Then the second doll was agitated: 'Hello, my name is Johnny.'

In the course of the experiment each doll stood next to one plate. On each turn, one of the dolls gave the child a 'clue' by 'saying,' for example, 'This plate has the penny under it.' The child then turned over the plate he thought was hiding the penny.

On each trial the two dolls and the two plates were equally distant from the subject. The two dolls spoke in randomly varied turns.

The clues incorporated six different terms: *here, there, this, that, close, far*. The doll providing the clue would say:

1. The plate over here has the penny under it.
2. The plate over there has the penny under it.
3. This plate has the penny under it.
4. That plate has the penny under it.

For the following two items an additional prop was used – a cup that served as a reference point for distance.

5. The plate close to the cup has the penny under it.
6. The plate far away from the cup has the penny under it.

It would have been possible to conduct the *close/far* tests using the speaker as the reference point (e.g. 'The plate close to me has the penny under it') and thus preserve comparability with the other items. I decided against this alternative for two reasons: it introduced a deictic factor into the test of comprehension of nondeictic terms, and it seemed to put inordinate strain on the fragile convention that one of the dolls, and not the experimenter, was speaking.

All subjects received each type of item twice, yielding a total of twelve items (see appendix D).

The experimenter experienced one methodological difficulty that reflects directly on the content of the experiment. It was very difficult, when providing verbal 'clues,' to suppress accompanying gestures. Overt pointing with the hands was easy to control. But covert pointing with the eyes could be suppressed only by the discipline of staring at some fixed point.

In ordinary speech, gestures accompany the concrete, location-indicating uses of the deictic terms. The experiment provided the children with an artificial, denatured message to interpret. One factor which may have rescued the messages from being conspicuously aberrant was that they were supposed to be coming from dolls, which ostensibly lack the means to point with either the hand, a nod of the head or a glance of the eyes.

## Subjects

The subjects were thirty-seven middle-class children drawn from two nursery schools in Urbana, Illinois and ranging in age from 2;6 to 5;3. They were divided into four age groups:

*Group* 1, n = 9, 2;6–3;4 (mean age 3;0)
*Group* 2, n = 9, 3;5–3;11 (mean age 3;8)
*Group* 3, n = 10, 4;1–4;8 (mean age 4;4)
*Group* 4, n = 9, 4;9–5;3 (mean age 5).

## Results

For each pair of words, there were more errors on the distal term than on the proximal one (see table 9). Subjects scored significantly better on *close* than on *far* (p <0.001, Sign test, 2-tail), and on *this* than on *that* (p = 0.05, Sign test, 2-tail). The difference between scores for *here* and *there*, although in the same direction, was small and not significant.

These results, however, do not necessarily indicate that there is an invariant order of acquisition in which the proximal term precedes the distal term. Some children did better on the distal terms. Table 10 shows the distribution of subjects achieving successful performance on

TABLE 9. *Demonstratives and deictic locatives. Errors[a] by word and by age*

| Group | Mean age (months) | this | that | here | there | close | far | Total |
|---|---|---|---|---|---|---|---|---|
| 1 | 36 | 6 | 8 | 5 | 8 | 4 | 13 | 44 |
| 2 | 44 | 3 | 9 | 5 | 4 | 3 | 10 | 34 |
| 3 | 52 | 4 | 3 | 5 | 5 | 2 | 8 | 27 |
| 4 | 60 | 0 | 5 | 1 | 1 | 0 | 1 | 8 |
| Total | | 13 (18%) | 25 (34%) | 16 (22%) | 18 (24%) | 9 (12%) | 32 (43%) | 113 |

[a] Maximum possible number of errors per word: 18 (Groups 1, 2, 4); 20 (Group 3).

TABLE 10. *Demonstratives and deictic locatives. Proximal–distal contrast*

| Group | Mean age (months) | Number of subjects achieving criterion on:[a] | | | | | | | | |
|---|---|---|---|---|---|---|---|---|---|---|
| | | *this only* | *that only* | *this and that* | *here only* | *there only* | *here and there* | *close only* | *far only* | *close and far* |
| 1 | 36 | 2 | 2 | 1 | 3 | 1 | 2 | 5 | 0 | 1 |
| 2 | 44 | 4 | 0 | 3 | 2 | 4 | 2 | 5 | 0 | 2 |
| 3 | 52 | 1 | 1 | 6 | 3 | 3 | 3 | 5 | 0 | 3 |
| 4 | 60 | 4 | 0 | 5 | 2 | 1 | 6 | 1 | 0 | 8 |
| Total | | 11 | 3 | 15 | 10 | 9 | 13 | 16 | 0 | 14 |

[a] Criterion: 2/2 correct on single terms.
4/4 correct on pairs.

one term in a pair, but not on the opposing term. The criterion for success on each individual word is two correct responses out of two. Another column indicates the number of subjects who achieve success on both members of a pair. Here the criterion is four out of four.

Close to equal numbers of subjects achieved success on *there* only and on *here* only. The ratio was 9:10. Thirteen children scored perfectly on both. For the *this/that* pair, more children achieved criterion on *this* before *that* than vice versa. The ratio of children succeeding only on *this* to those succeeding only on *that* was 11:3. Fifteen scored perfectly on both. For the *close/far* pair, the picture was different. Not a single child achieved criterion on *far* before achieving criterion on *close*. The ratio of children scoring perfectly only on *far* vs. those scoring perfectly only on *close* was 0:16. Fourteen scored perfectly on both.

What these data suggest is that children do learn *close* before *far*. There is a strong tendency for them to learn the contrastive meaning of *this* before *that*, but some children reverse this order. As for *here* and the contrastive sense of *there*, children are equally likely to learn either one first. It appears therefore that for the spatial deictic terms there is no invariant order of acquisition.

An interpretation in terms of perceptual strategies

Rank-ordering the words according to increasing number of errors produces the sequence shown here. The sequence has an onion-skin structure. The order of the three proximal terms that start the list is mirrored or reversed in the three distal terms that close it.

| | |
|---|---|
| *close* | 9 |
| *this* | 13 |
| *here* | 16 |
| *there* | 18 |
| *that* | 25 |
| *far* | 32 |

This pattern may reflect language comprehension, but it might also be due to a nonverbal perceptual strategy. Imagine that the children proceed by looking for the penny under whichever plate is most salient. In the *close* items a reference point is explicitly mentioned and therefore highly salient. Choosing the plate that is foregrounded by mention of

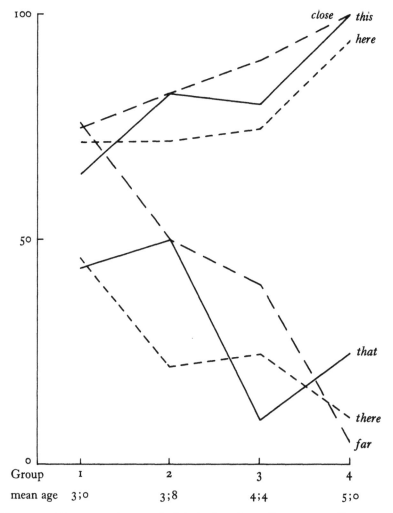

Figure 4. Demonstratives and deictic locatives. Percentage of responses proximal to speaker (*this/that, here/there*) or to point of reference (*close/far*)

the reference object leads to a correct response. In the *this* and *there* items no reference point is made explicit verbally. But the plate near the doll that is moving and 'talking' presumably receives more attention than the other one. Again, selecting the conspicuous plate leads to a correct answer.

Figure 4 shows the percentage of proximal responses made by subjects in the four age groups. For the deictic terms proximity is defined with respect to the speaker. For the nondeictic pair it is defined with respect to the point of reference made explicit in the message. Responses to the proximal terms, *close*, *this*, and *here*, are increasingly proximal (i.e. correct) with age. Responses to the distal terms are increasingly less proximal (i.e. correct). This then is a graphic representation of the peeling apart of the meanings of these two sets of terms.

In Group 1, responses to the proximal terms are already proximal above a chance level. And a distinction is evident between them and the distal deictic terms, because the scores for *that* and *there* hover at just about chance. In contrast, responses to *far* are not differentiated from responses to *close*. About 75 per cent of the responses to *far* instructions are proximal (i.e. errors). In the next age group, Group 2, this situation changes – proximal responses to *far* dropping to 50 per cent. While this is only what would be expected with completely random responding, it still reflects a differentiation between *close* and *far*.

In each of the three older groups, proximal responses (errors) to succeeding distal terms drop below chance level. In Group 2 it is responses to *there* that fall below chance level for the first time; in Group 3 it is responses to *that*; in Group 4 it is responses to *far*.

The difficulty of the distal items seems to be that children must override the tendency to select the hiding place that is salient in the situation. The more salient a hiding place, the more difficult it is to override the tendency to choose it. It is most difficult when a location, X, has actually been mentioned, as in *far from X*. It is somewhat less difficult when the distal deictic terms are used because no location has actually been mentioned by name. And it is less difficult when the distal term is *there* than when it is *that*. Apparently *there* signals a location away from the speaker more forcefully than *that* signals an entity that is away from the speaker. This may be because a speaker cannot ordinarily refer to his own current location as *there*, but can refer to an entity that is in the same location as himself as *that*.

If children perform well on the proximal terms and poorly on the distal terms, there is no way to determine whether their performance reflects a 'perceptual strategy' or comprehension of the proximal terms. Incontrovertible evidence of comprehension is provided only if the responses to both the proximal and distal members of a contrasting pair of terms are correct. Table 10 shows the number of children in each age group who achieved a perfect score on both terms of a contrasting pair. By this strict test it appears that a very small proportion of children in the youngest group understood the contrastive meanings of the terms. In the oldest group, every child comprehended at least one pair, but only three children (out of nine) gave evidence of comprehending all the pairs.

A further experiment could be constructed to determine whether the results are due to earlier comprehension of the proximal terms or to the perceptual strategy of selecting the more salient hiding place. It would be necessary to redress the saliency imbalance, or even shift it in the opposite direction, in favor of the distal terms. Instead of using two identical plates as hiding places, the distal ones should be more conspicuous, or perhaps larger, or gaudier. If performance still remains better for instructions using *this*, *here*, and *close*, then it is safe to infer that the difference reflects a real semantic priority of the proximal terms and not merely a perceptual strategy.

If, on the other hand, it emerges that performance is now best on the distal terms, then it will clearly have been a perceptual strategy that was responsible for the original results. Its general formula is: choose the more conspicuous hiding place. A subsidiary formula is: choose the hiding place that is near the speaker. And in this special case the perceptual strategy happens to be partly isomorphic with the semantic knowledge for which it is a substitute.

An excursion into production

With a small group of subjects an attempt was made to prompt the contrastive use of *this* and *that* and *here* and *there*. These children also carried out the Find-the-Penny task, but the clues were presented to them in such a way as to emphasize the contrasts:

1. This plate has a penny under it. That one doesn't.
2. That plate has a penny under it. This one doesn't.
3. The plate over here has a penny under it. The plate over there doesn't.
4. The plate over there has a penny under it. The plate over here doesn't.

After they had played the part of finder of the penny, the children were told that now it was their turn to hide it and to give me a clue.

Below are some examples of the clues the children gave:

Lynda (3;4)  5. The penny is not neath that plate; it's neath this plate. (Touching each plate in turn.)

           6. The penny is not neath the that; it's neath the this.

           7. It's neath the there.

           8. It's neath the that blue car.

           9. It's neath the that white one.

Clint (3;11)  10. That plate doesn't. That plate does.

           11. That one doesn't. That one does. (Pointing to each plate.)

Carole (4;3)  12. This plate has no dime under it but the other one does.

           13. The other one doesn't have a dime under it, and this one does. (Not correct. The plate near the speaker did not have the dime under it.)

           14. This one doesn't and this one does.

Ricky (4;9)  15. This one over here doesn't; this one over here does.

           16. This one over there doesn't have a penny. This one over here does.

Cindy (5;1)  17. This plate has a penny. That one doesn't.

           18. The one close by me has a penny. That one doesn't.

Sarah (5;1)  19. The plate over here has a penny under it. The plate over there doesn't.

           20. The plate over here has a penny under it. The plate far away doesn't.

Bianca (5;1)  21. The one over there, far away, has a penny. This one doesn't.

           22. The one over here has a penny. The one over there doesn't. (Without pointing.)

           23. This one has a penny. That one doesn't.

           24. The one over here has a penny. The one over there doesn't.

Example 5 shows knowledge that *this* and *that* can be used to contrast with each other, but does not reveal a grasp of the basis of the contrast, since the child touched each plate as she referred to it. Both plates, in effect, were equally near to the speaker.

Examples 6–9 by the same subject show that she had full awareness of the device I had been using to give clues and was heroically trying to use the same device, garbling it in the process.

Examples 10 and 11 show a contrast neutralized to *that one* vs. *that one*. And example 14, from a different subject, shows the complementary neutralization: *this one* vs. *this one*. Example 15 from yet another subject sets up a contrast between *this one over here* and *this one over here*. In all these examples, identification of the hiding place depends on actual physical pointing. The children do not exploit the deictic contrasts available in the language to supplement their gestural message. Example 16 incorporates one contrast, *here/there*, while neglecting the other, *this/this*.

The last three subjects, all just over 5 years of age, show productive mastery of the proximity–distance contrast inherent in *this* and *that* and *here* and *there*.

### The de Villiers & de Villiers experiment

De Villiers & de Villiers (1974) have conducted an investigation along very similar lines, but with several important differences in procedure and with results that provide interesting points of comparison. They investigated both comprehension and production of the following pairs of words: *my/your*, *this/that*, *here/there*, *in front of/behind*.

*Proximal vs. distal.* Although de Villiers & de Villiers were not concerned with which term of each pair, if any, is learned earlier, their data do have some bearing on this question. In general, their subjects' scores were higher on the distal terms than on the proximal ones. This pattern reverses the results of my experiment.

In the de Villiers comprehension experiment, the subject and the experimenter sat facing each other with a 'wall' between them. A cup was placed on each side of the wall and an M-&-M candy hidden under one of the cups. The children were told the location of the M-&-M in sentences incorporating the deictic expressions: e.g., 'The M-&-M is on this/that side, in front of/behind the wall,' etc. In this situation *that* and *there* happen to point to objects and locations that are near the addressee.

There are several observations to be made about the differences in the experimental setup and in the results.

First, the way *this/that* and *here/there* work in the de Villiers experiment can be considered to be a special case of their general meaning. What is nearer to the speaker is farther from the addressee and vice versa. Here the pattern becomes isomorphic with that of the *my/your* contrast.

The more general formulation is just that *this* and *here* are relatively closer to the speaker than *that* and *there*, without any necessary implication that the latter are closer to the addressee. My experiment tested children's knowledge of the more general formulation.

Contextual effects in children's comprehension of language have been well documented. For example, E. Clark (1972) has shown that young children who apparently understand the meaning of the preposition *on* in 'Put X on the table' fail to understand it when the instructions are, 'Put X on the cup.' They understand *on* as it applies to objects which function typically as supporting surfaces.

It is likely that the contradictory results obtained by this study and by de Villiers & de Villiers' do not reflect partitions in children's semantic systems, but rather a single perceptual strategy for dealing with the problem of finding the M-&-M or the penny. The application of the strategy yields different outcomes in the two experimental designs. In the de Villiers experiment the more salient hiding place is the one near the child. Choosing the salient cup will yield more correct responses for *that* and *there*. De Villiers & de Villiers do suggest (1974: 443) that 'the youngest children might merely have had a tendency to grab the cup nearest them.'

The combined findings support the argument presented above (pp. 87–90) for a conservative interpretation of results in experiments such as these. When performance is better on one member of a pair of contrasting terms than on the other, does it reflect the child's semantic development or contingencies of the experiment? Operationally the distinction is difficult to make. One can be completely confident that the child knows the *meaning* of the term that is first to be acquired only when he also knows the meaning of the term that is second to be acquired. Knowledge of the contrast rules out the possibility that the child is operating according to some pragmatic principle that bypasses the semantic system.

The extreme case where two similar but not identical experiments yield opposite 'orders of acquisition' for contrastive terms brings the problem into clear focus. But the same problem lurks when data are not contradictory. For example, in numerous experiments on acquisition of adjective pairs results have been interpreted to indicate that children learn the meaning of the unmarked term before they learn the meaning of the marked term. This may well be true, and is certainly plausible, but is not fully demonstrated unless the experiments have ruled out the possibility that the children are operating according to a pragmatic strategy that favors the unmarked term.

An ingenious method for investigating whether children's response patterns in such experiments could be attributed to perceptual strategies rather than to their interpretations of the tested lexical items was devised by Carey (1978). In addition to giving children task instructions with the targeted words (*more* and *less*), she gave parallel instructions with nonsense words: e.g. 'Would you please make it so I have more/less/tiv tea in here?' If the response pattern for *tiv* matches that for *less*, then the responses to *less* cannot safely be interpreted as reflecting the children's lexicons, but only as a response bias. The same, for that matter, holds true of responses for *more*. As Carey admits, there is a limitation in this method. If children show the same pattern of response for *tiv* as for *more*, one can only conclude that they *may* have been following a nonverbal pattern of preference for *more*. But one can't establish for certain that they were. So the question is left up in the air. No firm conclusions can be drawn.

An experimental format to distinguish between response biases and word comprehension might be constructed as follows. The usual format for tests of comprehension of adjective pairs is to show children two similar objects, e.g. a tall tree and a short tree, and to ask them to point out the tall one and to point out the short one. Responses to the 'tall' instructions are generally better than to the 'short' instructions. In the forced choice situation, errors necessarily involve making the opposite choice (see Brewer & Stone, 1975). To control for perceptual strategies, a third choice object should be introduced, intermediate between the other two on the critical dimension, but conspicuous for some irrelevant properties, e.g. a tree that's very broad, or decorated with Christmas decorations. If children have been making choices solely on the basis of miscellaneous criteria of saliency then they may well pick the gaudy middle-height Christmas tree in response to the instructions to point out the tall tree. If they still choose the tall tree then the inference is justified that they know the meaning of the word *tall*.

*Overall level of performance.* In general, subjects' scores were higher in the de Villiers experiment. If the difference in scores is robust, and if it is not due to differences in the subject population, it would mean that the children understood the *this/that* and *here/there* contrasts better in the special situation where distance from the speaker amounted to proximity to the addressee. This special form of the *this/that* and *here/there* contrasts corresponds to the contrast between the pronouns *I* and *you*, and its precedence suggests that the first-person–second-person, speaker–addressee contrast is an elementary deictic contrast.

Before jumping to this conclusion, however, other possible sources of the discrepancy in levels of performance must be ruled out. At least some of the difference seems to be due to experimental artifact introduced by differing criteria of success. In the de Villiers experiment, each child received each word only once. If we assume that at some age children are choosing at random in response to a word, then 50 per cent of them will be correct and 50 per cent incorrect if they are presented with that word only once. If they are tested on the same word twice, and the criterion for knowing it is being correct both times, then the number of subjects who choose 'correctly' will drop to 25 per cent. But if the children really do know the meanings of the words, scores should not drop radically with an increase in the number of times they are tested.

Table 11 shows the number of subjects choosing correctly in the de Villiers experiment and in my experiment. The data from my experiment are reported twice, once tabulating performance on two tests of each word, and once tabulating performance on only the first test of each word. In the two younger groups performance is considerably worse when two responses are tabulated. Therefore, in my experiment scores based on a single response are shown to be artificially inflated. By inference, scores for younger children may be inflated in the de Villiers experiment. The criticism no longer applies when scores approach 100 per cent correct.

In the presentation of their data de Villiers & de Villiers inadvertently boost their subjects' performance in still another way. Figure 1 of their report shows the number of subjects who responded correctly on each pair of terms in three conditions of their experiment. One curve is drawn for *this/that*, another for *here/there*, etc. However, the data points are based on children's responses to only one word within each pair, whichever happened to come first in an individual child's protocol. De Villiers & de Villiers do point this out, but the implications should be made explicit. The result of this procedure is that a figure which is the average of children's scores on *this* and *that* comes to appear as though it represents a score on the *this/that* contrast. To give an example of the discrepancy between these scores, let me perform the equivalent

TABLE 11. *Demonstratives and deictic locatives (comparison of de Villiers and Tanz results)*

| Group | Mean age (months) | | this | that | this and that | here | there | here and there | close | far | close and far |
|---|---|---|---|---|---|---|---|---|---|---|---|
| | | | | | | Per cent of subjects choosing correctly on: | | | | | |
| 1 | 36 | De Villiers (1 response) | 50 | 80 | | 30 | 88 | | | | |
| | | Tanz (1st response) | 67 | 44 | 22 | 78 | 44 | 33 | 78 | 22 | 22 |
| | | Tanz (2 responses) | 33 | 33 | 11 | 56 | 33 | 22 | 67 | 11 | 11 |
| 2 | 44 | De Villiers (1 response) | 80 | 91 | | 73 | 91 | | | | |
| | | Tanz (1st response) | 78 | 67 | 56 | 89 | 78 | 67 | 89 | 56 | 44 |
| | | Tanz (2 responses) | 78 | 33 | 33 | 44 | 67 | 22 | 78 | 22 | 22 |

| | | De Villiers (1 response) | | | | | | | | |
|---|---|---|---|---|---|---|---|---|---|---|
| 3 | 52 | | | | | | | | | |
| | | De Villiers (1 response) | 88 | 88 | 88 | 80 | 88 | 75 | 90 | 30 | 30 |
| | | Tanz (1st response) | 80 | 80 | 80 | 80 | 80 | 70 | 60 | 80 | 30 | 30 |
| | | Tanz (2 responses) | 70 | 70 | 60 | 60 | 60 | 60 | 30 | 30 | 30 |
| 4 | 60 | | | | | | | | | |
| | | De Villiers (1 response) | 90 | 90 | 80 | 100 | | | | |
| | | Tanz (1st response) | 100 | 67 | 67 | 100 | 67 | 67 | 89 | 100 | 89 |
| | | Tanz (2 responses) | 100 | 56 | 56 | 89 | 78 | 67 | 100 | 89 | 89 |

calculations for a segment of my data. In Group 1, 67 per cent of the subjects chose correctly for *this* (on their first response); 44 per cent chose correctly for *that*. The average for the two terms is 56 per cent. By the de Villiers method of representation, 56 per cent would appear as the percentage of children responding correctly on *this/that*. However the percentage who got both terms right was in fact only 22 per cent.

These methodological points are not meant as a criticism of the de Villiers experiment and do not invalidate their conclusions. At most they may retard the age of acquisition by half a year. The reason for making them is to demonstrate that the two experiments cannot be used to draw inferences about the comparative difficulty of their respective deictic frameworks.

Limited inferences can be drawn by comparing the de Villiers scores with my scores on the basis of first responses. When this is done (see again table 11), the disparities in overall performance appear to be erased. But more reliable inferences could only be made with more data from the de Villiers format: more responses than one for each word by each child, and a tabulation of success on contrasting pairs rather than just on the single terms.

*Points of view underlying the deictic terms.* According to the de Villiers analysis, *my/your*, *this/that*, and *here/there* are anchored in the speaker and in the speaker's location. To interpret them correctly, the hearer must adopt the speaker's point of view. For *in front of/in back of*, however, they claim that the directional 'information is usually given relative to the hearer, not the speaker' (p. 439). Therefore, no perspective shifting is required to comprehend *in front of/in back of*. This claimed difference is invoked to explain one of their findings. De Villiers & de Villiers report that performance on *in front of/behind* deteriorates with age. They reason that 'in the context of the game [the older children tend] to overgeneralize perspective changes from the other relative terms' (p. 444). In other words they erroneously interpret *in front of/behind* as though they were stated from the speaker's perspective.

But the analysis of *in front of/behind* seems to be questionable. In fact these positions can be defined from the hearer's point of view or the speaker's point of view or even from the point of view of a third party. (These possibilities have been discussed in greater detail in chapter 3.) An alternative hypothesis about the deterioration of performance takes into account this very property. The perspectives are variable.

Younger children are relatively unaware of the possibility of multiple perspectives. The older children become 'aware' that different points of view are possible when *in front of* and *behind* are used, and their scores drop to levels no better than random.

This hypothesis must be able to accommodate the fact that adults are not adversely affected by what is presumably as sophisticated an understanding of the possibility of multiple perspectives. Here the answer may be that the adults are more adept at analyzing which perspective will apply under what circumstances. Perhaps there is some rule such that the speaker *must* adopt the hearer's point of view if the two are directly contradictory. Additionally it should be noted that this is the only pair of terms on which adults did not score 100 per cent correct.

In the de Villiers study, *in front of/behind* is the most difficult pair of terms (except for the youngest children), *my/your* is uniformly the easiest, and *this/that* and *here/there* are in between. The full scaling could be attributed to the principle of the uniqueness of the point of view invoked. For *my/your*, the point of view is uniquely and exclusively that of the speaker. For *this/that* and *here/there*, it is again the speaker's, but not exclusively so. Sometimes the hearer is also included, and this occasional matching between the speaker's and hearer's perspectives makes the generalization that it is the speaker's point of view which is the critical one somewhat more difficult to discover. Finally, as was argued above, *in front of/behind* may be stated from different points of view.

## Possessive task

In another section of the experiment, the concept of possession was introduced. The reasoning was that children would naturally link proximity with possession. If they could override this association on the basis of verbal descriptions it would be strong evidence that they understood the proximal–distal contrast between *here* and *there*, etc. In this section, two new dolls were introduced, Peter and Susan. For each turn, they were described as owning two similar objects. For example, Peter and Susan each owned a chicken. In the tests of deictic terms, one object was placed close to Peter and the other close to Susan. Susan was always the 'speaker' in this section of the experiment. She identified the object that belonged to her and the one that belonged to Peter by saying, for example:

1. That chicken is mine, and this one is Peter's.

The experimenter then asked the child, 'Show me Susan's chicken.' The clues in this section were conjoined sentences, each one of them containing both members of a contrasting pair of terms, as in the example above. Each term was used once as the term in the initial clause, yielding a total of six items. The other five were as follows:

2. The pig over here is mine, and the pig over there is Peter's.
3. The car close to the house is mine, and the car far away from the house is Peter's.
4. This penny is mine, and that one is Peter's.
5. The spoon over there is mine, and the one over here is Peter's.
6. The plate far away from the cup is mine, and the one close to the cup is Peter's.

These six items were presented in the middle of the Find-the-Penny task, simply to relieve tedium.

Results

The number of errors for each word tested in the possessive task is given in table 12. Performance was significantly better on *this* than on *that* (p <0.001, Sign test), on *here* than on *there* (p <0.005, Sign test) and on *close* than on *far* (p <0.05, Sign test). In other words performance was better on each of the proximal terms than on its distal antonym.

In Groups 1 and 2, almost all responses for *this* and *here* were correct and almost all responses for *that* and *there* were incorrect. It seems clear that these children ignored the deictic contrast entirely and chose which object belonged to the doll, Susan, not on the basis of what she said, but simply on the basis of which object was closer to her. In Groups 3 and 4 the number of errors for *here* and *there* are equalized, suggesting that the children are no longer applying a uniform strategy of picking the object closest to the speaker but are attending to details of information in the verbal message.

In general, the tendency to select the object closer to the speaker was even stronger than in the Find-the-Penny task. Understandably so: the children were influenced by the reasonable assumption that proximity correlates better with possession than does distance.

TABLE 12. *Demonstratives and deictic locatives. Possessive task. Errors[a] by word and by age*

| Group | Mean age (months) | Word tested | | | | | | Total |
|---|---|---|---|---|---|---|---|---|
| | | *this* | *that* | *here* | *there* | *close* | *far* | |
| 1 | 36 | 1 | 7 | 1 | 8 | 2 | 7 | 26 |
| 2 | 44 | 1 | 8 | 0 | 7 | 4 | 7 | 27 |
| 3 | 52 | 0 | 4 | 2 | 2 | 2 | 3 | 13 |
| 4 | 60 | 2 | 5 | 3 | 3 | 2 | 1 | 16 |
| Total | | 4 (11%) | 24 (65%) | 6 (16%) | 20 (54%) | 10 (27%) | 18 (48%) | |
| | | $p < 0.001$ | | $p < 0.005$ | | $p < 0.05$ | | |
| | | (Sign test, 2-tail) | | | | | | |

[a] Maximum number of errors possible per word: 9 (Groups 1, 2, 4); 10 (Group 3).

Carter's longitudinal study of *here* and *there*

The difficulties of interpreting experimental data, and the realization that subtle differences in experimental format can yield results that reverse each other, suggest that it will be necessary to rely on the analysis of speech and comprehension in natural situations for corroboration of experimental results. In a finely detailed longitudinal study of the semantic development of one child, Anne Carter (1975) has documented the stages in his use of the deictic locatives. *Here* and *there* are first used by David without spatial significance. *Here* is invariably associated with gestures of reaching to give an object or obtain one. *There* is associated with the successful completion of actions. These initial action-bound meanings are apparently derived from the actions with which the words often occurred in adult usage.

Carter's study begins when David is 1 year old. At 19 months and 22 months, respectively, she records the first uses of *here* and *there* with spatial significance. At 20 months *where* is used on some occasions. Carter argues that at this point it is interchangeable with the developmentally prior *here*. At 24 months, David first uses *here* and *there* in the spatially contrastive sense of *near me* and *not near me*.

This finely delineated pattern supports the comparatively gross results of my experiment. The term that carries a proximal meaning in adult language is adopted first. Although, as Carter suggests, the contrastive sense of *here* as 'near me' cannot definitely be inferred to be present unless the child actually uses the word in contrast with *there* or some other expression signifying 'not near me,' it appears from her data that *here* in its locational sense was appropriately used for locations near the child. Of course if may be the case that David only made reference to locations near himself.

The finding from Carter's study that I take as being most directly corroborative of my experimental results is that the proximal term is the first to acquire spatial significance. Needless to say, evidence is needed from more children.

Dent (1971) offers evidence that is mixed with respect to the question of whether proximal or distal terms are the first to be learned. She attempted to elicit *here* and *there* and *this* and *that* from subjects aged 1;11 to 2;11. She succeeded in eliciting *here* from all of them, but failed to elicit *there* from 4 out of 18. On the other hand, she succeeded in eliciting distal *that* from more subjects (17) than proximal *this* (12). But even apart from this mixture of results, the data present obstacles to interpretation.

Dent used a question framework to elicit *here* and *there*, asking the children 'Where is X?' with X held within their reach (*here*) or out of their reach (*there*). She reports that the children who 'refused to produce the word *there*' (p. 4) would move to the object, touch it, and say *here*. She concludes that *here* is more 'readily produced' and proposes that this might be due to its possibly greater frequency in adult use. This line of reasoning illustrates a hazard that recurs frequently in research with children. Too direct an inference is made from children's behavior in an experiment to the underlying linguistic or cognitive organization that is the topic of investigation. In this example, the children's failure to use *there* need not be interpreted as a reflection of their knowledge of this word or on its accessibility at all. The children are asked where something is. The most effective way to identify an object or a location unambiguously is by getting close enough to be able to touch it and to say *here*. Again, as on many other occasions in these chapters, the neglected pragmatic factor intrudes, this time in the children's inter-pretation of the task they have been given, and through it, in their linguistic performance. If the researcher is not alert to the possibility of these 'intrusions' he may erroneously attribute their effects directly to linguistic competence.

Why are some unmarked terms not learned first? (Why are those that are learned first, learned first?)

Previous research (Donaldson & Wales, 1970; E. Clark, 1971, 1972, 1973a; Brewer & Stone, 1975) has shown that for many antonymic pairs of spatial adjectives, the unmarked term is learned before the marked term. The results of the present experiment show that for some other antonym pairs the generalization does not hold (see also Bower-man, 1979; Coker, 1978). Results for the deictic pairs *this/that* and *here/there* do not challenge the general rule as strongly as *far* (from)/ *close* (to), since, as was argued above, it is questionable whether they show the full marked–unmarked contrast. *Far*, however, does satisfy the criteria for 'unmarkedness' relative to *close*. And so it constitutes a test of the generality of the unmarked-before-marked hypothesis. In this experiment the marked term, *close*, appears to have been learned first.

Why are some unmarked terms learned before their marked counterparts and others not? By inquiring into this question we may be able to isolate the attributes of unmarked terms that account for prior acquisition in the set of antonym pairs for which this pattern does hold. Several properties, linguistic and cognitive, converge in the meanings of the unmarked words, *big, tall, long, deep*, etc. Which of these properties is responsible for their early acquisition relative to *small, short, shallow*, etc.? The strategy of the inquiry will be to examine how the pairs of terms relating to distance differ from these terms relating to size and how they are similar. We can conclude that the properties held in common are not responsible for the early acquisition of unmarked size terms. If we can discover some properties in which they differ, these will become candidates for explaining why *big* is learned before *small*, etc.

In his account of why the unmarked adjectives are learned earlier than their marked antonyms, H. Clark (1973) postulates that it is because they have fewer rules of application, or, in an 'equivalent hypothesis,' because they have fewer semantic features. It does seem plausible that it is easier to learn fewer of anything (including semantic features) than it is to learn more. However, we should recall that semantic features are not countable in nature. They are, after all, an artificial formalism. And as the comparison of Clark's and Lyons' feature analyses showed, one man's three-feature word is another man's one-feature word, and vice versa.

Furthermore, this version of why unmarked terms are learned first implicitly makes the claim that children learn relatively general and abstract meanings first and relatively concrete, specific ones later. There is no a priori reason to favor such a model. It does not accord with other patterns of progression in children's cognitive development. For example, in experiments on children's conceptual development using the technique of grouping objects it has been found that young children organize their groups around low-level concepts. If they are asked to create groups out of a collection of large red cubes, large blue balls, small blue cubes, and small red balls, they will separate out all four subsets rather than choosing the option of grouping all cubes together and all circles together, or all red objects together and all blue objects together.[1]

Unmarked terms do, however, have properties other than the length

---

[1] I owe this example of children's tendency to apply concrete specific concepts before general abstract ones to Ellen Markman.

of their feature specifications. By making comparisons with respect to these properties between the distance terms and those marked–unmarked pairs whose unmarked members are in fact learned first, we can discover more precisely why unmarked terms are sometimes learned earlier. At the very least we can eliminate some hypotheses.

Another characteristic of unmarked terms that might contribute to their early acquisition is actually one of their defining properties: the unmarked terms are used to discuss their respective bipolar dimensions per se and to direct discourse to the topic of these dimensions. So it is more likely that children's attention will be drawn to the appropriate dimension on occasions when the unmarked word is used than on occasions when the marked word is used.

As was discussed earlier, the unmarked terms *there* and *that* do not have any of these special uses. It is difficult to imagine how the child's exposure to the existential *there* would help him learn the meaning of the locative *there* which is only remotely related and appears to be much the simpler term anyway. Since *there* and *that* do not possess these special properties, the fact that they are not learned prior to their marked counterparts is still compatible with the proposal that unmarked terms possessing these properties are learned earlier precisely *because* they possess them. However, an examination of performance on the *far/close* pair weakens the hypothesis. *Far* does have some of the special uses hypothesized to facilitate acquisition. It does appear in neutral questions that direct discourse to the topic of distance (e.g. 'How far is the pharmacy?'). And yet *far* appears to be understood later than *close*. To the extent that the data are valid and reflect the subjects' semantic knowledge rather than their nonsemantic strategies for handling the experiment, we can conclude that the neutral use of the unmarked terms is not the determining factor in their early acquisition. Alternatively, the neutral use of the term may be a factor only when the whole dimension is already available to the child on a conceptual level (McNeill, personal communication). In the present case the distal pole of the proximal–distal 'dimension' may not be available.

A third property of unmarked terms is that in their contrastive sense they apply to the extended end of their respective dimensions. Perhaps it is this property which is implicated in the prior acquisition of those unmarked terms that *are* learned earlier. *Far*, like *long*, is the term for the extended end of its dimension. Procedures for measuring length and distance are identical, and H. Clark (1973: 38) treats the two dimensions as analogous. The young child, however, does not experience length and distance as measurable dimensions. And it appears to me that, from the point of view of children, the extended ends of the two dimensions will *not* be analogous. There is an important figure–ground distinction operating between them. Perceptually, length is a property of figures. Distance is a property of ground. In the ecology of the world of children, great length or height or width will make an object prominent. But distance will not make the spatial relation between two objects prominent. Instead, the converse is true. Great distance is in a sense the absence of relatedness in space. Proximity is the more basic and noticeable spatial relation. A relationship of proximity appears to be a 'better exemplar' (in Rosch's (1973) sense) of relatedness in space than is a relationship of distance.

Perhaps it is the term that refers to the best exemplar of a dimension that is learned earlier. For many dimensions – all those having to do with the size of objects – extension does define best exemplars. And the unmarked terms do tend also to be the extended terms. So for all those dimensions, the unmarked term will be learned first. For all dimensions where the extended term does not coincide with the best exemplar, acquisition order will follow the best examplar, and diverge from predictions made on the basis of which term is unmarked.

The concept of marked and unmarked does not apply to all antonymic adjective pairs in all languages. In the pair *old/young* in English, *old* is unmarked. One says, 'He is twice as old as she is,' and asks, 'How old are you?' but not 'He is twice as young as she is,' or 'How young are you?' In French, the marked–unmarked distinction applies to many spatial adjective pairs, but not to the adjectives relating to age. One cannot say, 'How old are you?' in French, but instead, 'What age are you?' ('What age do you have?')

These circumstances provide an opportunity for a further test of competing explanations of why some adjectives are learned before others. If they are learned prior to their antonyms because they are unmarked, then children learning a language in which they are *not* unmarked should not learn them earlier. If they are learned earlier directly for cognitive reasons, then they should be learned earlier across languages whether or not the marked–unmarked distinction applies.

There is a concept akin to that of 'best exemplar' employed in H. Clark's (1973) theory. It is the concept of 'perceptibility.' 'Perceptibility' is the criterion for designating one pole of a dimension as positive and the other as negative. Clark's prediction is that the term designating the positive pole will be learned first. 'Perceptibility' is very likely to correlate with best exemplars. But there are two drawbacks in the application of this concept. One is that Clark assumes that perceptibility coincides with extension, which, as I argued above, it need not. Second, the criterion of 'perceptibility' prejudges the grounds for best examplars. Sometimes these grounds may be functional rather than perceptual.

Reiterating the point made earlier in this chapter, the argument being presented here is not that proximal terms are learned before distal terms directly because proximity is a more basic concept. The relationship is indirect. The meanings of the proximal terms are more easily *discoverable* for the same perceptual reasons that make proximity the more basic concept. In other words, it is conceivable that a child has already grasped the concept of 'distance' as well as the concept of 'proximity,' but now, in the process of learning the meanings of words related to the two concepts, nevertheless maps out the words pertaining to proximity earlier – because they are easier to link to their corresponding concepts.

# 6 *Deictic verbs of motion: Easy* come? *Easy* go?

## The meaning of *come* and *go* and *bring* and *take*

The verbs of motion, *come* and *go*, have a directional component. The goal that defines the direction may be made explicit in a locative complement as in sentences (1) and (2):

(1) They went to Minneapolis.
(2) They came to Minneapolis.

But the direction is also specified by, and the choice of verbs constrained by, the location of the participants in the conversation. Therefore, the verbs incorporate a deictic component, and, as Fillmore (1966, 1971e) has pointed out, may be considered deictic verbs. Other verbs in this category are *bring* and *take*.

By a series of successive refinements, Fillmore arrives at the following account of the meaning of the deictic verbs:

*Come* and *bring* indicate motion toward the location of either the speaker or the addressee at either coding time or reference time or toward the location of the home base of either the speaker or the hearer at reference time. (1971e: 12)

To illustrate, sentence (3):

(3) Charlie is coming to the store on Friday.

is appropriate if the speaker or the addressee is at the store at the time of the utterance or expects to be there on Friday.

Fillmore adds the following extension to this basic definition:

*Come* and *bring* also indicate motion at reference time which is *in the company of* either the speaker or the addressee. (1971e: 17)

This accounts for the use of *come* in sentences such as (4):

(4) Is Alice coming with you?

when the destination is unknown or irrelevant.

Fillmore's final extension moves outside the sphere of speaker-addressee deixis proper:

*Come* and *bring* also indicate, in discourse in which neither speaker nor addressee figures as a character, motion toward a place taken as the subject of the narrative, toward the location of the central character at reference time, or toward the place which is the central character's home base at reference time. (1971e: 18)

This accounts for the use by one ordinary citizen to another (neither having high connections) of a sentence such as (5):

(5) So Solzhenitsyn isn't coming to the White House after all.

According to Fillmore, the destination of *go* is 'quite simply a place which is distinct from the encoder's location at coding time' (1971e: 9). These accounts of the meaning of *come* and *go* are not mutually exclusive. And, as Fillmore points out, there are situations where either one would be appropriate. Fillmore offers the examples in (6) and (7):

(6) He'll go to the office tomorrow to pick me up.
(7) He'll come to the office tomorrow to pick me up.

Either one of these sentences is appropriate if the speaker is not at the office at coding time.

Idiomatic uses of *come* and *go*

E. Clark (1974) has carried out an interesting extension of this analysis of *come* and *go* to include their widespread idiomatic uses. She adopts Fillmore's analysis of the destination of *come* as the DEICTIC CENTER. She argues that in idiomatic usage the deictic center becomes, instead of a physical location, a 'normal state of being,' or, in other cases, a desirable state. Idioms in which *come* is used to express a change of state describe changes that are in the direction of normality or in the direction of positively valued conditions. A paradigmatic example of the contrast between idiomatic *come* and *go* drawn from Clark's analysis is:

(8) Mortimer went out of his mind.
(9) Lovelace came back to his senses.

To a degree, Clark overstates her case. She claims that these verbs *invariably* imply movement in the hypothesized directions. Thus, she says that when the temperature is described as 'going,' whether up or down, what is implied is change away from the normal, or the desirable. She asserts that sentence (10):

(10) The temperature went down today.

allows only the interpretation that the weather got colder with the result of being less comfortable. This is not the case, as becomes evident if one acknowledges the acceptability of sentence (11):

(11) Phew. The temperature is finally going down.

Furthermore, there are idioms using *come* that indicate changes of state away from normal or desirable states:

(12) This dress is coming apart at the seams.
(13) The ribbon came undone.
(14) The cat came into heat today.
(15) That girl is going to come to grief.

Nevertheless Clark's argument is generally upheld.

To this analysis I would like to add two notations of my own. Clark mentions the pair *overcome* and *undergo*, commenting that the prefix *over* emphasizes the positive tone of *come* while *under* adds negative tone to *go*. The discussion offers an irresistible opportunity to publish a piece of free verse that I wrote several years ago:

(16) undergo
     overcome
     understand.[1]

Then there is the pair of deictic verb idioms having to do with bodily processes: the sexual *come*, and the scatological *go*, both applicable, if not equally, to movement toward normal and/or desirable states.

The experiment discussed below does not take into account these idiomatic uses of the motion verbs. The reason they are included in this discussion is to indicate that the central meanings of *come* and *go* and *bring* and *take* are not the only meanings children encounter. Whether

[1] According to R. Jakobson, paronomasia, 'a semantic confrontation of phonemically similar words, irrespective of any etymological connection, plays a considerable role in language.' Here the confrontation is between morphologically similar words: *under*, *over*, *under*, and *go*, *come*, *stand*.

the existence of these extended uses affects the decodability of the central uses is a question that has not yet been answered, and that should be borne in mind.

Especially in the idiomatic uses, but also in the core nonidiomatic ones, there is a great deal of dialect variation on *bring* (Fillmore, personal communication), and this makes the total picture more complicated, both for children and for investigators of child language. Children may be exposed to varying models. Ideally, the investigators should ascertain which ones. In this study, where parental speech and speech in the community were not sampled, it will be assumed that the input to the children followed the general pattern outlined by Fillmore and described above.

## A study of children's comprehension of the deictic anchoring of *come/go* and *bring/take*

Procedure

The subject and the experimenter were seated side by side at a small table. On the table was an 8 × 14 × 6 inch box made of masonite, closed on five sides and with its open side facing toward them. This was a 'house.' A wooden flight of steps ran up the outside from the level of the table to the level of the top of the box. Two dolls representing people were standing inside. Two others were standing on top (see figure 5).

The experimenter told the child, 'This is a house and these are the people who live in it. Here's the upstairs, and here's the downstairs. This is the inside and this is the outside. Sometimes one person tells another one to do something. And then the other one does it. When they talk they do what they did the other time.[1] Like this: "Jump up and down" [a doll upstairs is agitated]. And then somebody else does it [a doll downstairs jumps up and down]. Now I'm going to tell you some more things that they said, and you're supposed to make one of them say it, and then make another one do it.'

There were four locations that could be referred to: upstairs, downstairs, inside, outside. And four verbs were tested. Combining these in all possible ways yielded a total of sixteen test items of the following type:

1. Come upstairs and take a bath.

[1] For some children the convention had been established that a doll who was 'speaking' was made to move (see p. 83 above).

2. Bring a key outside.
3. Take a penny downstairs.
4. Go inside and turn off the light.

For a complete listing, see appendix E. Each verb was tested a total of four times.

Before each new item was presented, the dolls were set up in appro-

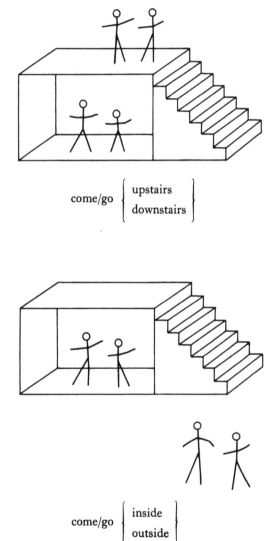

Figure 5. Deictic verbs. Diagram of experimental set-up

priate positions. For 'inside' or 'outside' items, two dolls were placed inside the house on the 'main floor,' and two were placed outside. For 'upstairs' or 'downstairs' items, two dolls were placed upstairs and two downstairs. Two dolls were necessary at each location to accommodate all possible combinations of speaker and addressee locations: one in one location, the second in the other, or both in the same location.

For the *bring* and *take* items, miniature objects were made available for the dolls to 'bring' or 'take'. These objects were duplicated and placed in all relevant positions so that their position would not restrict the children's choice of speaker and addressee. For example, if the instructions were, 'Bring a penny downstairs,' then a penny was available both upstairs and downstairs.

In the majority of comprehension tests, children are required to give a nonverbal response. This was also the case in the *back/front/side* study and the *this/that/here/there* study reported above. In this experiment, however, the children were asked not merely to point to the speaker and the addressee but to enact their roles. The reason for doing this was not to place an extra burden on the children, but to give them an opportunity to check themselves by hearing themselves *say* 'Come upstairs' or 'Go upstairs' from a particular position. In imagining what my own procedure would have been as subject in an experiment about where one must be to say *come* and where one must be to say *go*, the spontaneous procedure seemed to be covert rehearsal of the relevant phrase in various positions. By asking the children actually to utter the instructions I felt I was prompting them to 'rehearse' in a similar manner, albeit overtly.

Several aspects of the children's responses were recorded: if they changed the instructions in repeating them, how they changed them; which doll was selected as speaker; which doll was selected as addressee; and where either or both of the dolls moved in the course of the transaction.

The simplest correct responses are as follows: for *come* and *bring* instructions, the speaker should be one of the dolls located in the place mentioned in the instructions, for example for 'Come upstairs . . .,' the speaker should be upstairs. For *go* and *take* instructions, the speaker should be one of the dolls that is not in the place mentioned. The addressee, who is being asked to change his state, should presumably never be in the place mentioned. He can't come upstairs or go upstairs if he already is upstairs.

There are cases, however, where it may be appropriate to choose a doll that is not in the place mentioned as the speaker of *come* and *bring* instructions. A doll who is downstairs *can* appropriately be selected to say 'Come upstairs.' Whether this choice is correct depends on what the doll does next. If it does nothing, then the response is scored as incorrect. But if the speaker accompanies its addressee upstairs, then its response is counted as correct.

It is also possible to address *bring* instructions to a person who is already in the place mentioned in the instructions. A doll who is inside can say to the other doll who is inside, 'Bring a pine cone inside.' The addressee must then go outside to get the pine cone and return with it.

In this experiment, the children's knowledge was tested only on the core of the contrast between *come* and *go* and between *bring* and *take*. Some of the disjunctive conditions of Fillmore's definition were compressed into single conditions. First, in the situation represented in the experiment, the position of the addressee for *come* and *go* instructions was constrained by the destination mentioned in the test items. A message to come or go upstairs was now presumably addressed to some person who was downstairs. Therefore, it was only the location of the speaker that was relevant to the choice of *come* vs. *go*. And while the general definition of *come* and *bring* states that they indicate motion toward the speaker or hearer, in this context they only indicated motion toward the speaker.

Second, since the reference time of all the test items was the present, there was no difference between reference time and coding time. Therefore the children were not being tested on their knowledge of the disjunctive condition that *come* and *bring* indicate motion toward the speaker or the addressee at either coding time *or* reference time. One would expect that knowledge of the relevance of future locations would be acquired later than knowledge of the relevance of contemporaneous locations.

Subjects

The subjects were twenty-eight children from nursery schools in Champaign, Illinois, aged 2;11 to 5;3. They were divided into four groups of unequal size but of approximately equal age span:

*Group* 1, n = 5, 2;11–3;5
*Group* 2, n = 6, 3;6–3;11
*Group* 3, n = 8, 4;1–4;7
*Group* 4, n = 9, 4;8–5;3.

## Results

Addressee choice

A message either to go upstairs or to come upstairs is presumably addressed to someone who is *not* upstairs. Pragmatic considerations select the appropriate addressee. The particular verb used is not discriminative. Therefore, the children's choices of addressee did not reflect their understanding of the meanings of the deictic verbs. For this reason, the analysis which follows will be based on speaker choice.

In any case, errors in addressee choice were quite rare. (There were only twelve errors in the entire test, although there were additional instances in which children failed to identify an addressee by neglecting to have anyone carry out the instructions.) When errors in addressee choice did occur, they were difficult to interpret. For example, subject no. 10 (age 3;2) carried out item no. 3 ('Take a penny downstairs') by making a doll downstairs say it (incorrect speaker) and making the other doll downstairs execute it. The addressee carried a penny upstairs. The addressee choice is incorrect, but the error reflects a misunderstanding or neglect of 'downstairs' more than misunderstanding of the deictic verb.

Clark & Garnica (1974), in a study discussed below, were able to evaluate addressee choice as a function of the deictic verb by using some nonimperative messages of the type, 'I'm coming upstairs,' or 'Can I come upstairs?' and asking the child to indicate the addressee of these messages.

Speaker choice

*All deictic verbs.* An age group (4) × verb (4) repeated measures ANOVA was performed on the data. The main effect for verb was significant, ($F_{3,81}$ = 19.690, p <0.001). Performance was significantly better on *go* than on *take*, and better on *take* than on *come* or *bring* which were not significantly different from each other (Student–Newman–Keuls procedure, p <0.05). There was no significant main effect for age.

The percentage of correct speaker choices for each verb in each age group is shown in table 13. The percentages are calculated in two ways, once as a proportion of total possible responses; and once as a proportion of the responses that could be scored as either correct or incorrect. This procedure was adopted because a number of data points were lost in one of several ways. The two youngest subjects and one older subject failed to complete the test. In some cases children made a doll carry out the instructions, but failed to make a doll issue them. In other words, there was no speaker at all. In other cases, the child changed the verb in the instructions, for example from *come* to *go*. These responses were eliminated in the overall tally. It did not seem appropriate to judge the choice of speaker according to the original verb. The responses of verb reversal will be discussed separately below.

Because some responses could not be scored as either correct or incorrect, the scores for correct and incorrect responses are not complementary. It is possible for a child to have at once more correct responses to *go* than to *come*, and more incorrect responses to *go* than to *come*. If it happened that children made more scorable responses on *go* than on *come* (for whatever reason), then higher scores on *go* might reflect merely that difference, and nothing about comprehension of restrictions on the use of these terms. But in fact the number of scorable responses was fairly evenly distributed across terms. Out of a possible total of 112 responses for each verb, there were 86, 98, 89, and 85 to *go*, *come*, *take*, and *bring*, respectively. Selective loss of data, therefore, is not likely to have contributed to the pattern of the results. But in

TABLE 13. *Deictic verbs. Percentage of correct speaker choices by word and by age*

| Age | Verb | | | | Mean |
|---|---|---|---|---|---|
| | *go* | *come* | *take* | *bring* | |
| Group 1 | 77 (50)[a] | 44 (40) | 36 (20) | 50 (30) | 52 (35) |
| Group 2 | 100 (79) | 29 (21) | 89 (67) | 26 (21) | 62 (47) |
| Group 3 | 75 (56) | 57 (50) | 50 (44) | 69 (56) | 62 (52) |
| Group 4 | 93 (78) | 43 (42) | 75 (67) | 46 (36) | 64 (55) |
| Mean | 87 (67) | 45 (39) | 65 (52) | 49 (38) | |

[a] X (Y). X: Ratio of correct responses to responses which can be scored correct or incorrect. (Y): Ratio of correct responses to total possible responses.

order to rule out this possibility conclusively, separate statistical tests were carried out on error scores and scores of correct responses.

No child scored correctly on all sixteen test items. The highest proportion correct for any individual was fourteen out of fifteen. The results indicate that full knowledge of the deictic component of *come* and *go* and *bring* and *take* has not been achieved at age 5.

*Deictic directions.* Although overall the percentage of correct responses was only at chance level (on any trial, two dolls out of four were correct speaker choices), performance was not random. In every age group, the number of correct responses was higher for *go* than for *come* (p <0.01, Sign test, 2-tail). Performance was also generally better on *take* than on *bring* (p <0.05, Student–Newman–Keuls procedure). The results of tests on errors corroborate the results based on correct responses. There were fewer errors on *go* than on *come* (p <0.001, Sign test, 2-tail). And there were fewer errors on *take* than on *bring*, although these results did not reach significance (p = 0.264, Sign test, 2-tail).

The age by verb interaction complicates these findings. In two age groups there were more correct responses on *take* than on *bring*; in two other age groups there were more correct responses on *bring* than on *take*. What makes these results especially difficult to interpret is the fact that the age groups in each pair are nonadjacent. Groups 1 and 3 do better on *bring*; Groups 2 and 4 do better on *take*. It is not clear why this is the case.

*Go* and *take* as a pair showed significantly fewer errors than *come* and *bring* (p = 0.01, Sign test, 2-tail). Comparing them in terms of correct responses, they showed more correct responses than *come* and *bring* (p <0.05, Student–Newman–Keuls procedure).

*Causatives.* Turning now to a comparison of the basic terms of motion with their causative counterparts, the differences between them are not significant if they are examined pair by pair, *come* and *go* vs. *bring* and *take*. However, the difference between *go* and *take* is significant. There were more correct responses for *go* than for *take* (Student–Newman–Keuls procedure, p <0.05). And there were significantly fewer errors for *go* than for *take* (p <0.002, Sign test, 2-tail). *Come* and *bring* showed no difference. But scores for both *come* and *bring* were no better than chance. To determine whether the addition of a causative component to meaning of words adds a uniform increment of complexity, it would be necessary to test children who are *older* and achieving a better score on at least one word in the pair.

When the responses of the individual children are examined, certain patterns emerge that strengthen the impression given by the overall analysis. For each pair of terms, *come* and *bring* on the one hand, *go* and *take* on the other, three response profiles are possible. A child may have a high level of correct responses, an intermediate level, or a low level. Intermediate scores probably reflect random responding. A low score reflects systematic error. Permuting these three profiles for the two pairs of terms, nine categories of responses are generated. Table 14 shows the number of subjects from each age group who fell into each of these nine categories. And table 15 provides more detailed information, giving actual scores for the subjects in each category.

A majority of the subjects (17 out of 28) are distributed in the three categories where *go/take* show a high proportion of correct responses (categories 7–9). The remainder all fall into the *go/take* random categories (categories 4–6). And most of these seem to perform at random on *come/go* as well. The three categories where *go/take* scores are low are empty categories (categories 1–3).

Four out of five children in the youngest group are in the totally random category (category 5). None of the children in the oldest group can be found there.

A substantial number of subjects fall into the category of high *go/take* scoring combined with low *come/bring* scoring (category 7). What this category represents is a uniform pattern of response treating *come* as identical with *go*, and *bring* as identical with *take*. The most striking example of this pattern is subject no. 41 (age 5;3) who made eight out of eight correct speaker choices for *go* and *take*, and zero out of eight correct choices for *come* and *bring*. His speakers were never at the destination mentioned in the message.

Six subjects fall into the category of high *go/take* scores and random *come/bring* scores (category 8). This category represents at least a differentiation between the two sets of terms even though the meanings of *come/bring* have not been fully consolidated. Subject no. 15 (age 3;6) provides a good example. He made seven out of seven correct speaker choices for *go* and *take*, and three out of six for *come* and *bring*.

Four subjects, two from each of the two oldest groups have high scores on both sets of terms (category 9). These four subjects appeared to know the deictic distinctions between *come* and *go* and between *bring*

TABLE 14. *Deictic verbs. Response categories by age*

| | | | | | | | | | |
|---|---|---|---|---|---|---|---|---|---|
| | Number of subjects in response category | | | | | | | | |
| go/take: | 1 low | 2 low | 3 low | 4 random | 5 random | 6 random | 7 high | 8 high | 9 high | Total |
| come/bring: | low | random | high | low | random | high | low | random | high | |
| **Age** | | | | | | | | | | |
| Group 1 | 0 | 0 | 0 | 0 | 4 | 1 | 0 | 0 | 0 | 5 |
| Group 2 | 0 | 0 | 0 | 0 | 0 | 0 | 3 | 3 | 0 | 6 |
| Group 3 | 0 | 0 | 0 | 1 | 4 | 1 | 0 | 0 | 2 | 8 |
| Group 4 | 0 | 0 | 0 | 0 | 0 | 0 | 4 | 3 | 2 | 9 |
| Total | 0 | 0 | 0 | 1 | 8 | 2 | 7 | 6 | 4 | 28 |

TABLE 15. *Deictic verbs. Scores of individual subjects grouped in response categories*

| Category go/take | come/bring | Subject Number | Age | go/take Correct | Errors | come/bring Correct | Errors |
|---|---|---|---|---|---|---|---|
| 1 low | low | — | | | | | |
| 2 low | random | — | | | | | |
| 3 low | high | — | | | | | |
| 4 random | low | 30 | 4;6 | 3 | 4 | 0 | 7 |
| 5 random | random | 7 | 3;1 | 1 | 1 | 3 | 2 |
| | | 10 | 3;2 | 4 | 4 | 2 | 4 |
| | | 12 | 3;3 | 4 | 2 | 3 | 5 |
| | | 14 | 3;5 | 4 | 2 | 3 | 5 |
| | | 24 | 4;1 | 4 | 2 | 1 | 2 |
| | | 27 | 4;3 | 4 | 2 | 4 | 1 |
| | | 29 | 4;5 | 1 | 3 | 4 | 3 |
| | | 31 | 4;7 | 4 | 4 | 4 | 4 |
| 6 random | high | 6 | 2;1 | 1 | 1 | 3 | 0 |
| | | 25 | 4;3 | 4 | 2 | 6 | 2 |
| 7 high | low | 17 | 3;8 | 5 | 0 | 1 | 5 |
| | | 20 | 3;10 | 7 | 1 | 1 | 7 |
| | | 21 | 3;10 | 4 | 0 | 0 | 4 |
| | | 34 | 4;9 | 4 | 0 | 1 | 5 |
| | | 36 | 5;1 | 4 | 1 | 0 | 4 |
| | | 37 | 5;1 | 6 | 1 | 2 | 5 |
| | | 41 | 5;3 | 8 | 0 | 0 | 8 |
| 8 high | random | 15 | 3;6 | 7 | 0 | 3 | 3 |
| | | 18 | 3;8 | 6 | 1 | 2 | 3 |
| | | 22 | 3;11 | 6 | 0 | 3 | 4 |
| | | 33 | 4;9 | 7 | 1 | 5 | 3 |
| | | 35 | 5;0 | 6 | 2 | 3 | 4 |
| | | 40 | 5;3 | 6 | 2 | 3 | 4 |
| 9 high | high | 23 | 4;1 | 5 | 2 | 7 | 1 |
| | | 28 | 4;4 | 6 | 1 | 8 | 0 |
| | | 32 | 4;8 | 5 | 2 | 7 | 1 |
| | | 38 | 5;1 | 6 | 0 | 7 | 1 |

and *take*, at least as these terms applied within the framework of this experiment.

The distribution of children in these categories suggests that the path to an understanding of the distinction between *come* and *go* and between *bring* and *take* usually leads through correct use of *go* and *take* first. This is not a universal course, however. There were two children who appeared to be learning *come*, or *come* and *bring* before *go* and *take* (category 6). One of them was in fact the youngest subject, for whom data are drastically incomplete. It is only tentatively that she can be placed in any category at all. But of her three responses for *come* instructions, all three were correct. She has no score at all for *bring*. It is tempting to place her in the random category simply because otherwise her protocol and that of one other child are the only ones to challenge the strong generalization that emerges in the rest of the data. But it seems more prudent to interpret her performance as an indication that the generalization is not absolute.

*Verb reversal.* Occasionally, in making a doll issue the instructions, a child changed the verb, for example, from *come* to *go*. More than half of the subjects in the three younger groups did this at least once. But they did not do it often. Verb reversals occurred in only 7–8 per cent of responses in these three groups. In the oldest group only two out of nine subjects reversed a verb, and verb reversals totalled only 1 per cent of all responses.

Each of the four verbs tested was subject to change. *Come* was changed to *go* three times; *go* to *come* four times; *bring* to *take* three times; and *take* to *bring* eleven times. *Take* was changed a disproportionately large number of times.

Out of a total of twenty-one verb changes, eleven were followed by responses that were correct for the new verb. Ten were incorrect for the new verb.

A possible way to interpret verb reversals is that they reflect non-distinct codings on the part of children. Children may readily switch *come* to *go* in imitation if the terms are synonymous for them. This interpretation is compatible with the 50 per cent level of correct speaker choice for the changed verbs. If the children did not know the distinction between the verbs then they may have chosen the speaker at random and have made a correct choice 50 per cent of the time. But careful scrutiny of which children committed verb reversals makes the interpretation dubious. Among them were three of the four children who otherwise showed evidence of knowing the distinction between *come* and *bring* and *go* and *take* by scoring at a high level on both pairs of terms. The fact that they also reversed verbs suggests that the reversal did not reflect an identity in underlying semantic codings, but was merely an effect of task repetition. The older children appeared to be less susceptible to this kind of confusion. Verb reversals correlate more strongly with age than with general success on the task.

*Special strategies.* Under the experimental conditions there was one way in which a speaker could appropriately say 'Come to X' despite the fact that he was not located at X at the time. That was if the speaker then proceeded to accompany the addressee to the location. One subject (aged 4;9) used this option twice for *come* instructions. She chose a doll that was outside to say 'Come inside and eat lunch.' Then that doll and the other outside doll proceeded to go inside together. This subject also chose a doll that was upstairs to say 'Come downstairs and watch TV.' The speaker then joined the addressee in going downstairs.

### The Clark & Garnica study

Clark & Garnica (1974) also conducted a study of children's acquisition of *come* and *go* and *bring* and *take*. They predicted that *come* and *bring* would be correctly understood before *go* and *take* and concluded that their findings supported this prediction. My findings, once again, with perverse consistency, contradict theirs. Attempting to disentangle these contradictions is a complicated procedure. I will proceed by discussing first the theoretical basis of their predictions, then their experimental procedure as compared with mine, and finally their actual data.

*Theoretical considerations.* Clark & Garnica predict that *come* and *bring* will be learned before *go* and *take* on the grounds that children learn the meaning of positive members of positive–negative pairs first. They argue that *come* and *bring* are positive because the 'conditions that have to be met for the use of [these verbs] are all positive in form.' 'For *come*, the speaker or addressee is at the goal at the time of the utterance or at the time referred to in the utterance . . . [For *go*] the speaker is not at the goal at the time of the utterance' (p. 560).

The broader framework of the theory of semantic development elaborated by E. Clark and by H. Clark generates a different prediction. Elsewhere they have argued that the unmarked term of a marked–unmarked pair will be the first to be acquired. In many cases the marked–unmarked distinction and the positive–negative distinction coincide, with the unmarked term also being the positive one. However, as I argued in chapters 3 and 5, this is not always the case. And, in fact, the two distinctions do not coincide in the deictic verbs. The verb *go*, which Clark & Garnica identify as negative, is the unmarked member of the *come/go* pair as the following evidence will attest.

*Go* is the neutral verb of motion because it can be used in ways that ignore the direction of motion with respect to the speaker and addressee. For example, sentence (17) applies to a runner if he is moving rapidly toward the speaker and the addressee as well as away from them or in any other direction.

(17) Look at him go!
(18) Look at him come!

Example (18) is appropriate only if the runner is moving toward the speaker.

In addition to ignoring direction of motion, *go* can subsume both directions, toward and away from speaker and/or hearer, simultaneously, as in (19e). But *come* is awkward in this context (see 19d).

(19) a. All the people were coming in.
　　 b. All the people were going out.
　　 c. The people were coming in and going out.
　　 d. ?The people were coming in and out.
　　 e. The people were going in and out.

Both of the examples offered so far are marginal in that they rely on idiomatic expressions. The sentences in (20) are nonidiomatic and analogous with sentences that test the markedness of other dimensional adjectives by examining whether they can be used in neutral questions.

(20) a. Do you want to come to a movie?
　　 b. Do you want to go to a movie?

Example (20a) presupposes that the speaker is going to the movies. Example (20b), through its illocutionary force as an invitation, may imply that the speaker is going to the movies, but it does not presuppose it. It can appropriately be uttered if the speaker is not going, but it is not restricted to that condition. According to Bierwisch's (1967: 8) heuristic principle that 'a sentence is the less normal the more conditions outside of it have to be met for it to be acceptable,' sentence (20b) is more 'normal' than sentence (20a), and hence, *go* is unmarked relative to *come*.

Extrapolating from other research by E. Clark and by H. Clark, this analysis suggests that *go* should be acquired before *come*. While this prediction matches the results of my experiments, I cannot confidently invoke the principle of markedness as an explanation because, as I showed in chapter 5, it does not correctly predict order of acquisition across all word pairs.

Unfortunately, Clark & Garnica overlook the applicability of the markedness hypothesis to the deictic verbs. And so they do not offer their perspective on what might be expected to occur when these two hypotheses, unmarked precedes marked, and positive precedes negative (both promulgated by E. Clark and H. Clark, and usually compatible), come into conflict.

*Differences in experimental procedure.* The experimental procedures in the Clark & Garnica study and in my own study have in common a basic framework, but they also have numerous differences. Both use the device of asking children which of several figures can be the speaker of a certain utterance. The Clark & Garnica study asks this question explicitly. My task requires children to make a similar judgment without asking the question explicitly. Both probably put greater demands on subjects than comprehension tasks usually do, in that they demand responses which are, to differing degrees, meta-linguistic. Cromer (1971) used a similar task in his study of the acquisition of temporal structures. He showed subjects a sequence of events in pictures, and asked when in the sequence it was possible for a person in the pictures to make various temporally marked comments.

The Clark & Garnica design is more complete than my own. It includes items in which the subject is supposed to identify the speaker and others in which the subject is supposed to identify the addressee. In my experimental design the subject identifies speaker and addressee for each item, but the choice of addressee is not constrained by the deictic verb used. It is constrained instead by the destination. Only a person who is downstairs can be asked either to *come upstairs* or to *go upstairs*. So the subject's choice of addressee does not reflect upon his comprehension of the deictic verbs. In the Clark & Garnica procedure there are three animals participating in discourse, each located in a different place. For some items the experimenter identifies the speaker and the subject must choose one of the other two animals as the addressee. For other items the experimenter identifies the addressee and the subject must choose the speaker.

The Clark & Garnica study also uses a broader range of sentence types in the messages that are exchanged between the various animals. My study employed imperative sentences exclusively. The Clark & Garnica study employed questions (requests for permission) and declaratives, both first- and third-person, as well. The items in my study correspond most closely to the items in Clark & Garnica's Sp-1 category where the message is a command, and the role to be identified is that of speaker. A residual difference of this most closely comparable task is that Clark & Garnica asked children to indicate 'Which animal can say to the bear: "come into the house"?' Questions about who *can* say something or whether something *can* be said are meta-linguistic in nature. Other research has shown that children's meta-linguistic knowledge lags behind the corresponding linguistic knowledge. In my study, the children were asked actually to make one of the dolls issue the command. Doing this may also require meta-linguistic knowledge but the balance of meta-linguistic and ordinary language skills tapped by the two tasks might be slightly different.

Finally, there is no overlap in the age distributions of the subjects in the two studies. Clark & Garnica's subjects are 5;6 to 9;5. Mine are 2;11 to 5;3.

*Further interpretations of the data*. The conclusion that Clark & Garnica arrive at is that *come* and *bring* are acquired earlier than *go* and *take*. They qualify this generalization, however, by stating that 'whenever the speaker had to be identified, it was easier overall if the verb was *go* or *take*; when the addressee had to be identified, it was easier with *come* or *bring*' (p. 568). They do not offer an explanation for this result. If we probe further into their data and analyse this discrepancy in a different way, some tentative explanations do emerge, and some additional insight is provided into how children carry out this task.

The distinction that Clark & Garnica refer to in the quotation above, between performance when the speaker had to be identified and when

TABLE 16. *Deictic verbs. Clark & Garnica, 1974: table 1 (Instructions used with deictic verbs in four situations)[a]*

| Verb | Situation | | Role to be identified |
|---|---|---|---|
| *come/go* | Sp-1 | Which animal can say to X: 'Come into the Y?' | Speaker |
| | Sp-2 | X is walking to the Y. Which animal can say to *you*: 'X is coming into the Y?' | Speaker |
| | Ad-1 | X says: 'Can I come into the Y?' Which animal is he talking to? | Addressee |
| | Ad-2 | X says: 'I'm coming into the Y.' Which animal is he talking to? | Addressee |
| *bring/take* | Sp-1 | X has a Z. Which animal can say to X: 'Bring the Z into the Y?' | Speaker |
| | Sp-2 | X has a Z. X is walking to the Y with the Z. Which animal can say to *you*: 'X is bringing the Z into the Y?' | Speaker |
| | Ad-1 | X has a Z. X says: 'May I bring the Z into the Y?' Which animal is he talking to? | Addressee |
| | Ad-2 | X has a Z. X is walking to the Y with the Z. X says: 'I'm bringing the Z into the Y.' Which animal is he talking to? | Addressee |

[a] X = one of three animals (lion, pig, monkey; dog, bear, rooster). Y = one of four goals (house, pool, barn, garden). Z = one of six miniature portable objects (racquet, flag, bottle, drum, piano, truck).

TABLE 17. *Deictic verbs. Based on Clark & Garnica, 1974: table 2 (Percentage of correct responses to each situation according to the verbs used)*[a]

| Situation | Role to be identified | Verb | | | | Mean |
| | | *come* | *go* | *bring* | *take* | |
|---|---|---|---|---|---|---|
| Sp-1 | Speaker | 92 | 72 | 85 | 66 | 79 |
| Sp-2 | Speaker | 54 | 69 | 51 | 73 | 62 |
| Ad-1 | Addressee | 97 | 15 | 92 | 20 | 56 |
| Ad-2 | Addressee | 90 | 44 | 81 | 38 | 63 |
| Mean | | 83 | 50 | 77 | 50 | |

[a] Each percentage based on 132 data points.

the addressee had to be identified, reflects a prior collapsing of types of items in their test. There are two types of items requiring speaker identification, and two types of items requiring addressee identification. Table 16 (reproduced from Clark & Garnica, 1974: table 1) lists examples of each type of item. Table 17 (based on Clark & Garnica, 1974: table 2) indicates the percentage of correct responses for each type of item according to the verb used. The response patterns do not show merely a two-way differentiation, between speaker items and addressee items, but a four-way differentiation. Each type of situation elicits a different response pattern. And, in fact, performance on Sp-1 (one of the speaker items) shows more commonality with Ad-2 (one of the addressee items) than it does with Sp-2, in the sense that performance is better on *come* and *bring*. What can account for these variations?

In three of the situations, Sp-1, Ad-1, and Ad-2, there are more correct responses to *come* and *bring* than to *go* and *take*. In the fourth situation, Sp-2, the reverse is true, and *come* and *bring* drop to chance levels of correctness. The most extreme differential between *come/bring* and *go/take* occurs in situation Ad-1. For *come* and *go* the ratio of correct responses is 97:15; for *bring* and *take* it is 92:20. There are more correct responses to *come* and *bring* and at the same time more incorrect responses to *go* and *take* than in any other category. The instructions for these items are as follows:

1. X says: 'Can I come/go into the Y?' Which animal is he talking to?

2. X has a Z. X says: 'May I bring/take the Z into the Y?' Which
   animal is he talking to?

X is asking for permission to enter the goal. Children overwhelmingly
designate the animal at the goal as the addressee of the question. Why?
Perhaps because they take it to be the custodian of the goal and therefore
the appropriate individual to give permission. This would mean that
even if children know the core of the semantic distinction between *come*
and *go*, etc., as their best performance (on Sp-1) suggests they do, the
semantic rules they hold are flexible enough or weak enough to be
overriden by pragmatic considerations.

The question of why the response profile is inverted in Sp-2 (*go*
better than *come* and *take* better than *bring*) remains a puzzle. What is
unique about Sp-2? One distinctive aspect of this situation is that the
addressee of the message is supposed to be the child himself. The instructions are:

3. X is walking to the Y. Which animal can say to *you*: 'X is coming/
   going into the Y?'

Presumably the reason the instructions were formulated in this way is
that if the animals were speaking one to the other, both of them would
have to say 'X is coming into the Y,' and neither could say 'X is going
into the Y.' The animal at the goal would have to say 'X is coming'
because X is moving toward the place where the animal itself is located.
The animal who is not at the goal would also have to say the same thing
because X is moving toward the place where its addressee is located.
Sp-2 is also distinctive in that the subject of the message is the third
person, X, rather than *I* and *you*. After these differences have been
clarified, however, it remains unclear how they could contribute to a
reduction in correct responding to *come* and *bring*. That is the phenomenon that requires explanation, since the scores for *go* and *take* are not
radically different from what they are in Sp-1. The following suggestion
is speculative. One animal is supposed to be reporting the move-
ments of another animal, X. Let us say that the speaker is in the
barn. If X is moving toward the speaker, the speaker would ordinarily
say 'X is coming' or 'X is coming here' rather than 'X is coming into
the barn.' The goal would be omitted entirely or indicated by using the
deictic locative *here*. Perhaps the very fact that the speaker *names* the
destination contributes to the child's impression that the speaker is

not located in it. Therefore, the child tends to identify the speaker as *not* being at the goal. The paradoxical proposal is that the child's very sensitivity to the normal ways of expressing deictic coordinates may lead to incorrect responses for *come*.

If the responses in the Ad-1 situation (very high on *come*, very low on *go*) are temporarily eliminated from consideration on the grounds that they reflect a pragmatic judgment on the part of the subjects and not a semantic judgment, then the difference between *come* and *go* scores is considerably reduced. When Ad-1 scores are included, the ratio of correct responses to *come* and *go* is 83:50. The Ad-1 scores excluded, the ratio is reduced to 79:62. When Ad-1 scores are included, the ratio of correct responses for *bring* and *take* is 77:50. Eliminating Ad-1 scores, it is 72:59. Under this analysis, the difference between scores on the 'positive' and 'negative' verbs is reduced. But the residual difference is still in the opposite direction from my results.

What, in either experiment, could account for an artificial skewing of results in favor of either *come* or *go*? Clark & Garnica acknowledge that children might have a tendency to choose the animal at the goal because of the prominence of the goal in the message. This strategy would make a child appear to understand *come* and *bring* correctly, and misunderstand *go* and *take*.

Another strategy followed by some children, according to Clark & Garnica, is to choose the animal at the goal when it is the addressee who is to be found, and the animal outside the goal when it is the speaker. It is questionable, however, whether this can be called a strategy or merely a recapitulation of the data. The concept of a strategy can be usefully invoked to explain children's responses in a language acquisition experiment if it suggests some compelling logic the children are following that happens to bypass the linguistic knowledge under investigation. There is compelling logic, for example, in placing objects *inside* containers and *on top of* supporting surfaces. Verbal instructions apart, boxes are to put things in, tables to put things on. Therefore it is plausible to postulate as E. Clark (1973b) did that children simply followed this procedure in tests of comprehension of prepositions rather than distinguishing *in* from *on*. There is no comparable compelling logic in choosing animals at the goal as addressees and animals outside it as speakers. Even as a summary of the data, this formulation is questionable. As was pointed out earlier, it obscures differences in children's responses to different categories of speaker items.

If subjects in the Clark & Garnica experiment were susceptible to the first strategy, simply choosing the animal at the goal, why didn't the subjects in my experiment operate with a like strategy? This question is the more pressing since Clark & Garnica report that in a pilot study *all* the younger children (age 4;0 to 5;0) employed this strategy. The different response requirements of the two experiments provide a possible explanation. Making a doll actually say the sentence with *come* or *go* may have provided a check against rote responding. When the required response is merely to point at or to name an animal, it is easier casually to select the more prominent. This is likely to be the one in the place mentioned. Without the experimentally induced 'rehearsal' of the phrase in question as coming from one or another doll, it is harder to select on any basis other than prominence. Even if the child 'knows' how to use *come* and *go* in spontaneous speech, he may not know how to tap this knowledge in order to answer the meta-linguistic question 'Who can say P?' or 'Who can he say P to?'

Alerted to the ubiquity of unexpected artifacts, I combed my experiment for the presence of any reciprocal biases in favor of correct responses to *go* and *take*, and I found something that might be one. In the format of my experiment, the speaker and the addressee may either be in the same location or in two different locations. The simplest correct scenario for *go* and *take* has them both in the same place. For example, one person who is downstairs tells the other person who is downstairs to 'Go upstairs.' In contrast, the simplest scenario for *come* and *bring* has the speaker and addressee in different places. The corresponding example is of a person who is upstairs telling a person who is downstairs to 'Come upstairs.' The children appeared to know the elementary fact that in order to move upstairs, a person must first be downstairs. So it was established that the addressee of 'Go upstairs' and 'Come upstairs' was a person who was downstairs. Now if there should be a tendency to have the speaker be a person in the same place as the addressee, perhaps because it is easier to imagine or to represent two people talking together when they *are* together, then the child will appear to understand *go* before *come*. This strategy, if it exists, is a much more complicated one than the strategy of choosing the animal at the goal, and probably does not even represent an economy over the application of real semantic criteria. It is not a parsimonious account of the data. Nevertheless, it may exist and be a contaminating element. The Clark & Garnica study does not admit of interference by this strategy since the arrangement of the three animals each in a different location ensures that the members of every speaker–addressee pair will be in two different places.

To rule out the effects of this hypothetical strategy and at the same time bypass the goal-choice strategy that contaminates the Clark & Garnica results, a hybrid experiment might be carried out. The arrangement of materials would come from Clark & Garnica, with the three participating figures each in different locations. The subject would be required to make the speaker 'say' the message and to make the addressee carry it out or respond to it, as in my experiment. I think it would also be desirable to use messages that are embellished by activities other than *coming* and *going*, for example 'Come to the barn and eat some hay,' rather than just 'Come to the barn.' The isolation of the word tested does not seem to facilitate the child's comprehension of it. On the contrary, it is probably easier to enter into the roles of speaker and addressee, and 'try out' the appropriateness of different animals to fill those roles, when the message has some enlivening detail. The desired effect, again, is to lessen the meta-linguistic flavor of the task. At the very least, these embellishments will probably help to make the subjects persevere in the task.

As they currently stand, the combined results of the two experiments are inconclusive. Other research on the use of deictic verbs in early spontaneous speech claims to show acquisition of *go* before *come*, but the demonstrations are not compelling. Keller-Cohen (1973) examined the occurrence of these verbs in 8-hour samples of speech by 3 year old children. She reports that 'the number of children who used *take* more frequently than *bring* was significantly greater than those who used *bring* more frequently than *take*,' and similarly for *go* and *come*. Although she interprets this as confirmatory evidence that *go* and *take* are less complex for children than *come* and *bring*, little can actually be inferred from these data. Frequency of occurrence alone does not necessarily reflect degrees of complexity or order of acquisition. *Go* also occurs more often than *come*, and *take* more often than *bring*, in adult speech (cf. Jones & Wepman, 1966), where frequency is presumably a function of contextual requirements rather than of semantic complexity. Frequency in adult speech does not directly determine frequency in child speech, but the contextual factors that govern frequency in one are likely also to affect the other. Keller-Cohen also cites several other studies that report similar frequency rankings for the deictic verbs, and two diary studies that report *go* as entering the lexicon earlier than *come*, and (in one study), *take* appearing several months before *bring*.

Dent (1971) carried out a more critical examination of the deictic verbs in early speech. She attempted to determine whether children use them appropriately, that is contrastively. Her subjects were in the age range 23–35 months. She interacted with them to elicit *come/go, bring/take, here/there*, and *this/that*. More children used the word *go* in their interaction than used the word *come*, and no child used *come* who did not also use *go*. The picture was more evenly mixed for *bring* and *take*. The same number of children used them. Incidentally, more children used *bring* and *take* than used *come*. One is reluctant to infer from this that *bring* and *take* are 'acquired' before *come*. In the face of this reluctance, the data are revealed to be incapable of compelling any conclusion.

## Causative and noncausative verbs

In addition to predicting that *come* and *bring* would be learned before *go* and *take*, Clark & Garnica predict that within the pairs *come* would be learned before *bring* and *go* before *take*. They base their predictions on the interpretation of *bring* and *take* respectively as the causative forms of *come* and *go*.

In English the prototypic causatives are verbs which without modification can be either intransitive or transitive. Lyons (1968) uses the example *move* as in (21) and (22):

(21) The stone moved.
(22) John moved the stone.

*Move* in (22) is 'causative' because it applies to John's causing of the effect that the rock moved. Other examples of causative verbs are: *melt, open, warm*, etc. There is another category of causative verbs that are not identical to their intransitive (adjectival) counterparts, but morphologically related, for example *legalize (legal), enrich (rich), harden (hard)*. A third category of causative verbs are lexically distinct from their noncausative counterparts. Some examples of these 'suppletive' causatives include *kill* (cause to die), *show* (cause to see), *give* (cause to have or get), and the current topics of interest, *bring* (cause to come), and *take* (cause to go).

Clark & Garnica propose that *bring* and *take* (and other causative verbs) will be learned later than their noncausative counterparts because they are more complex in meaning, 'including' as they do the meaning of the noncausative along with the additional semantic element 'CAUSE.'

*Does 'bring' mean 'cause to come'?* It is considered an accident of the lexicon that some predicates in English do not have a single-word causative counterpart, for example 'cause to disappear', 'cause to like' or 'cause to hear.' It is also considered an accident that some causatives involve zero-modification of their noncausative counterpart, others morphological modification, and others lexicalization. Lyons observes, for example, that English might have expressed *John killed Bill* as *\*John died Bill*.

But there may be a degree of systematicity in the distinction between zero-modified causatives and lexicalized causatives. Let us examine a set of causative–noncausative pairs in both of these categories testing the relationship between the causative and a paraphrase of the form 'cause to___.' *Melt*, for example, is very close in meaning, perhaps synonymous with *cause to melt*. However *show*, which Kastovsky (1973) and others describe as the causative of *see*, is not precisely synonymous with *cause to see*. The latter implies a degree of achieved success that the former does not. In example (23), the conjoined clause asserting failure makes the sentence a contradiction, but sentence (24) is not contradictory.

(23) He caused her to see her mistake, but she failed to see it.
(24) He showed her her mistake, but she failed to see it.

By contrast, *cause to melt* and *melt* (transitive) equally imply that the object actually melts.

As with *show/see*, *feed* is not precisely synonymous with *cause to eat*. It has the additional meaning of 'supply with food.' If a doctor tells a woman on a strict diet that she must eat and succeeds in persuading her, he is *causing her to eat*, but he is not *feeding* her.

Perhaps then the fact that some causatives are morphologically related to their intransitive counterparts (e.g. *open*) while others aren't, is not an arbitrary fact of English, but is semantically motivated. The proposal is that suppletive causatives often involve some change of meaning beyond the addition of the CAUSE component. Morphologically related causatives do not introduce comparable changes of meaning.

It should be noted however that there is another possible 'motivation' for the morphological nonidentity of *feed* and *eat* or *show* and *see*. *Eat* and *see* are already optionally transitive. If they also had a causative reading there would be ambiguity in expressions like *John saw Bill*. It could mean either what it currently means or that *John made Bill see*. And it would be possible to say about a man who had just left to give his pet some dogfood, *John went home to eat his dog*.

How do these observations apply to the deictic verbs? *Come* and *go* do not occur as transitives. So there is no threat of ambiguity to hinder their candidacy for use as causatives. Yet their causative counterparts are the lexically distinct *bring* and *take*. Is *bring* synonymous with *cause to come* and *take* with *cause to go?* The following examples suggest that they are not.

(25) They brought the dead man into the basement.
(26) ?They caused the dead man to come into the basement.

The discrepancy between the two sentences comes about because *come* attributes to its subject a degree of volition which does not apply to the object of *bring*.

The generalization that *come* implies volition must be qualified in several ways. First, *come* seems to have a volitional component only when its subject is animate. In sentences (27) and (28):

(27) The mail came.
(28) The rain came in the window.

the subjects are inanimate, and the action of coming is nonvolitional. *Bring* may be construed as the causative counterpart of this version of *come*.

Second, the volitional element in *come*, even with an animate subject, is not absolute. It is not contradictory, for example, to say (29):

(29) The man came unwillingly.

But there are apparently degrees of volition, as can be seen by comparing (29) with (30):

(30) The man was brought unwillingly.

In contrast with the man in (30), the man in (29) seems to arrive with some residue of willingness. He came under his own steam if not by his own wishes.

Moving now in the opposite direction, *cause to come* cannot always be paraphrased as *bring*. Sentence (32) means something slightly different from sentence (31):

(31) The king caused the princess to come to the window.
(32) The king brought the princess to the window.

Sentence (32) seems to have the sense that the king went to the window with the princess, while sentence (31) does not. For this reason, sentence (34), an extension of (32), is a contradiction, but (33), which is derived from (31), is acceptable.

(33) The king caused the princess to come to the window, but he didn't come himself.
(34) ?The king brought the princess to the window, but he didn't come himself.

In this case *bring* seems to carry an implication of accompaniment. The subject causes the object to come or to arrive, but he does so by coming too. This meaning is not captured in the representation of *bring* as 'CAUSE to come.' Sentence (33) could however be paraphrased as:

(35) The king sent the princess to the window.

*Send* can be considered a second causative counterpart to *come*, one which does not entail accompaniment (E. Clark, personal communication). Fillmore (1971e: 10) has noted the various modulations in the meaning of *bring* and captures them in his distinction between 'the *enabling*, the *conducting*, and the *conveying* senses of "bring."' He explains that the sentence '"A brings B to C" is paraphrasable as either "A enables B to come to C," or "A comes to C with B accompanying him," or "A comes to C conveying B."'

*The debate over the generative semantics analysis of causatives.* It appears, then, that some lexical causatives are not strictly synonymous with their noncausative counterparts. In some cases (e.g. *show/see*) the causative actually seems to lack a component of meaning present in the noncausative (i.e. the achievement of seeing). In other cases the causative has additional components of meaning other than just CAUSE. *Come* and *bring* appear to be mixed cases.

The preceding discussion of synonymy between causative verbs and their noncausative counterparts is separable from the debate between generative semanticists and lexicalists over the former's analysis of causative verbs. Fodor (1970), arguing for the lexicalist position, states that 'phrases [such as *cause to die*] will exhibit distributional characteristics which differ from those even of words with which they are synonymous' (p. 436). The debate does not center on the presence or absence of synonymy but on how to *represent* meaning relationships in a grammar.

According to the proposal advanced by the generative semanticists G. Lakoff (1970a) and McCawley (1968, 1971), the meaning of a causative verb incorporates the meaning of its intransitive or adjectival counterpart plus the abstract semantic element CAUSE. More crucially, they argue that these are organized as a complex hierarchical tree containing at least two underlying clauses, one with the cause predicate and one with the effect predicate. For a sentence such as *The bartender melted the ice* the clauses correspond approximately to the 'bartender cause X' and 'X: ice melt.' For a sentence like *David killed Goliath* the clauses correspond to 'David cause X' and 'X: Goliath become dead.' The crux of the generative semantics position is first, that word meanings are not atoms but molecules constituted of more elementary semantic units and second, that these units are organized in complex structures which are not in principle different from the underlying structures of sentences. In the case of the causatives, the crux is the claim that a single surface verb like *melt* or *kill* really consists of at least two predicates. One type of evidence offered for the two-predicate analysis of causatives like *melt* has to do with the ambiguity of sentences like (36) (Fodor, 1970):

(36) Floyd melted the glass and that surprised me.

What's surprising might be either that Floyd melted the glass (the reading of sentence (37)) or that the glass melted (the reading of sentence (38)).

(37) Floyd melted the glass though it surprised me that he did.
(38) Floyd melted the glass though it surprised me that it did.

The fact that the pro-form, *that*, in sentence (36) can apply to either proposition is taken as evidence that both of them appear in the underlying structure of the sentence.

Fodor (1970) has presented some arguments against the causative analysis. First he questions the comparability of suppletive causatives like *kill* and causatives that are identical to their noncausative counterparts. The two categories, he argues, do not have the same type of syntactic relation with the noncausative. Sentence (39) is not ambiguous in the same way as (36). The only thing that can be surprising in sentence

(39) is that John killed Mary (the reading in sentence (40)) and not that Mary died (the reading in sentence (41)).

(39) John killed Mary and that surprised me.
(40) John killed Mary though it surprised me that he did.
(41) *John killed Mary though it surprised me that she did.

Fodor goes on to argue that even for morphologically identical causative–noncausative pairs the generative semantics analysis does not hold. He states that the causative *melt* is not derived from the same underlying structure as 'cause to melt.' One of his items of evidence has to do with the acceptability of (42) and the unacceptability of (43):

(42) Floyd caused the glass to melt on Sunday by heating it on Saturday.
(43) *Floyd melted the glass on Sunday by heating it on Saturday.

As Fodor puts it, 'one can cause an event by doing something at a time which is distinct from the time of the event. But if you melt something, then you melt it when it melts' (p. 433). The arguments continue back and forth. The debate is not over whether there is a relationship between transitive *melt* and intransitive *melt*, or between *kill* and *die*, but over how the relationship should be represented in a grammar.

*Child language and the causative analysis.* Research in child language has had little direct bearing on the selection of grammars in linguistic theory, but Bowerman's (1974) fascinating analysis of causative over-extensions by children is informed by the generative semantics analysis of causatives, and according to her, lends it support.

At the age of 24 months, Bowerman's daughter, Christy, began to use numerous verbs causatively which are not causative in adult English. For example:

(44) (Playing a musical toy) I'm singing him ( = making him sing).
(45) (Pulling a bowl closer to her as she sits at the kitchen counter) I come it closer so it won't fall ( = make it come closer; bring it closer).

Bowerman reasons that Christy must have discovered that verbs like the transitive *open*, *break* and *melt* are related to their intransitive or adjectival forms and that she is producing novel causatives on analogy with these legitimate ones. By themselves these observations are non-committal with respect to competing analyses of the structure of causative verbs. The fact that a child recognizes the relations between the transitive and intransitive forms of these verbs does not imply that the generative semantics analysis of the relation is correct. The relationship could be captured in a variety of ways by other types of grammars.

However, another finding adduced by Bowerman does seem to offer support for the psychological reality of the causative analysis. At the same time that Christy began to produce novel causatives she also started to use sentence patterns that combine two propositions. Bowerman cites several ways of combining: juxtaposition, conjoining, embedding. Some examples are given below:

(46) Want out see wow-wow. ('I want to go out to see the dog.')
(47) Find girl fall down. ('Let's find the picture where the girl falls down.')

Repeating a point made earlier, the generative semantics analysis of causatives claims that a simple sentence with a causative is derived from an underlying structure with at least two propositions. Christy's over-extended use of causatives indicates that she has grasped the structure of causatives. What is striking is that this achievement seems to coincide with the development of the ability to combine propositions by various 'syntactic' means as well. Of course this could just be a coincidence. Data from other children will be required to decide whether the simultaneity is accidental or reflects a single psycholinguistic step forward.

*Semantic complexity and order of acquisition.* Having discussed some qualifications to the statement that *bring* is synonymous with *cause to come*, let us return to the implications of the statement for language acquisition. Clark & Garnica (1974), it will be recalled, expected that *bring* and *take* would be learned later than *come* and *go* because they contain an additional component of meaning.

The proposal that children learn the meanings of words by gradually adding features or 'components' seems to presume that at some level they must have abstracted the relevant features or components before they can use a word appropriately. Applied to the problem of causative verbs, the model suggests that children must have acquired the component CAUSE before they can understand verbs such as *bring* or such as *open* in its transitive sense.

Bowerman's (1974) model is somewhat different. She suggests that children first learn the meanings of *bring* and *open* (transitive) as global 'unanalyzed' terms. Subsequently they become 'aware' of the internal structure of these verbs. As evidence for the transition, Bowerman offers the data on her daughter's overextended use of a causative principle. Some examples were given above ((44) and (45)); another follows:

(48) (M about to put baby in high chair for lunch; baby needs a diaper change) No, mommy, don't eat her yet ( = don't feed her yet), she's smelly!

Earlier, Christy had used only legitimate causative verbs causatively. Having discovered that 'make the door open' and 'open the door' are different ways of saying the same thing, Christy hypothesized that a different way to say 'make her eat' was 'eat her.' The proliferation of causative overextensions suggests to Bowerman that something has changed in the child's semantic system – that the element CAUSE has now been abstracted out of the global meanings of words and has become available for manipulation.

In Bowerman's model the child can and does use (produce and comprehend) certain causative verbs before having abstracted out the semantic primitive CAUSE. In the feature model, as I understand it, the semantic primitive must already be available in order for causative verbs to be used appropriately. Also, because the structure of the causative verb is more complex than that of the corresponding noncausative, the feature hypothesis predicts it will be harder for the child to acquire. Bowerman's discussion does not make such a commitment, and leaves open the possibility that a causative verb could be learned before or simultaneously with its noncausative counterpart.

More data on the acquisition of causative–noncausative pairs can select between these two models. Evidence that the noncausative verb is invariably learned before its causative counterpart would support the Clark & Garnica hypothesis. Evidence that they are sometimes learned in the inverse order or simultaneously would support Bowerman. Reiterating an earlier point with respect to the Clark & Garnica results, it would be valuable to know whether *go* is always learned before *take* and *come* before *bring*. Looking outside the category of deictic verbs, are other noncausatives learned before their causative counterparts – *see* before *show*, *learn* before *teach*, *have* before *give*? And outside the category of suppletive causatives, among morphologically identical causative–noncausative verb pairs such as *open* or *break*, do children always learn the intransitive, noncausative sense before the transitive, causative one? Production data may have some bearing here, even if they are not conclusive. Taking the example of *open*, do children invariably begin by using *open* to describe states of affairs ('The door is open'), or intransitive actions ('The door opened')? Confirmatory evidence on this question would support the Clark & Garnica hypothesis. Or are children equally likely to begin with causative uses ('He opened the door'; 'Open the door')? In that case Bowerman's interpretation would be favored.

*Speaker specification and addressee specification.* As was mentioned earlier, my study was limited to children's knowledge of the *come/go* distinction and the *bring/take* distinction in the circumscribed situation where only the speaker's current location was relevant to the selection of the correct verb. The Clark & Garnica study was also limited to *current* locations, but was broader in that it tested children's knowledge of the relation between verb choice and addressee location as well as speaker location. And it yielded some suggestive data with respect to the comparison of these latter two factors. Referring to table 17, we can compare the percentage of correct responses (to all verbs combined) when the problem is to identify the addressee, and when the problem is to identify the speaker. The mean percentage of correct responses for all items requiring choice of the speaker is 71 per cent. The mean percentage of correct responses for all items requiring choice of the addressee is 60 per cent. This overall comparison suggests that children grasp the importance of speaker location for choice of deictic verbs before they discover the equal relevance of addressee location. A further examination of Clark & Garnica's results lends more support to this conclusion.

Departing from their analysis of group trends in the data, Clark & Garnica also examined the patterns of individual children's responses. On the basis of this individual analysis they identified four different strategies for responding. Because the 'strategies' correlate with ages Clark & Garnica suggest that they may be sequential stages. Some of these strategies were referred to earlier. They are set out in complete form below:

Strategy A: Choose the animal at the goal for both the speaker and the addressee.

Strategy B: Identify the speaker with the nongoal, while still identifying the addressee with the goal.

Strategy C: For *come*, identify the speaker with the goal and the addressee also; for *go*, identify the speaker with the non-goal and the addressee with the goal.

Strategy D (adult-like responses): For *come*, identify speaker and addressee with the goal; for *go*, identify both with the nongoal.

Viewed as strategies these are rather puzzling. It is hard to understand *why* a child would follow a strategy like B or C. But if the strategies are viewed instead as simple summaries of data and then scrutinized anew a possible interpretation emerges. One important detail unifies Strategies A, B, and C. The pattern of response for addressee location in all three groups is similar: very high scores on *come* and *bring*, scores considerably below chance level on *go* and *take* (see table 18 where the relevant figures are in bold type). These polarized scores reflect the fact that the children uniformly, whatever the verb, identified the addressee as being at the goal. Formulating the strategies on the basis of responses to both speaker and addressee items for one verb at a time obscures this commonality. Looking at response patterns for speaker items and addressee items separately across verbs allows it to emerge. What the pattern

TABLE 18. *Deictic verbs. Clark & Garnica, 1974: table 4 (Percentage of semantically correct responses produced by each group)[a]*

| Group | Speaker | | Addressee | | Mean |
|---|---|---|---|---|---|
| | *come* | *go* | *come* | *go* | |
| A | 90 | 24* | **100** | **1*** | 54 |
| B | 30* | 80 | **73** | **23*** | 52 |
| C | 76 | 87 | **94** | **33*** | 73 |
| D | 83 | 90 | 94 | 70 | 84 |
| | *bring* | *take* | *bring* | *take* | |
| A | 89 | 22* | **100** | **0*** | 52 |
| B | 38* | 79 | **73** | **14*** | 51 |
| C | 70 | 87 | **88** | **22*** | 66 |
| D | 88 | 96 | 93 | 91 | 90 |

[a] Figures that are consistently below 50 per cent are marked by an asterisk; bold type is my addition.

suggests is that the children were not yet actively exploring different links between the deictic verb and the location of the addressee. Faced with the task of identifying the addressee they seem to have adopted a consistent pragmatic strategy that altogether bypasses the choice of verb used: when in doubt, pick the animal at the place mentioned. By contrast the connection of *come* and *go* with the location of the speaker was construed differently by children following Strategies A, B, and C. It appears that it was being actively explored. By the time children were following Strategy C, they had the connection figured out.

Tracing Fillmore's progress in specifying the meanings of the deictic verbs, we find a similar sequence. The first two in the series of seven successive hypotheses he proposes to account for the meaning of *come* and *bring* refer only to the location of the speaker. Perhaps this is not a coincidence, but reflects the fact that certain elements of these semantic structures are more easily accessible to child and linguist alike. It will be interesting to discover whether the correspondence continues further. Fillmore adds the factor of addressee location before adding the factor of reference time. If children also adhere to this order, then we will be well advised to investigate the basis of Fillmore's intuitions.

Even if the child's knowledge of the meaning of the deictic verbs unfolds step by disjunctive step, each step cannot be totally independent of succeeding steps. If the child's first 'hypothesis' about the meaning of *come* and *bring* refers only to speaker location, then it must have been made in the face of certain exceptions that do not fit a rule so stated. Temporarily neglected information about the possible relevance of addressee location still must interfere with the formulation of a hypothesis that focuses exclusively on speaker location.

There is one joint syntactic–pragmatic context in which the applicability of *come* and *bring* is uniformly based on speaker location and not on addressee location. This is the present-oriented imperative. *Come to X*, with the present as the understood reference time, invariably indicates that the speaker is at X. In contrast, *John is coming to X* or *Is John coming to X?* leave open the alternative possibilities that it is the speaker *or* addressee who is at X. The imperative imposes the constraint that the moving party is to be the addressee himself. If the addressee were clearly specified as the party in motion in a declarative sentence (*You are coming to X*) or in a question (*Are you coming to X?*) then by process of elimination, it would have to be speaker location that determined the choice of *come* or *go*. Clark & Garnica's results indicate that children make by far the greatest number of correct responses when the message containing the deictic verb is an imperative. Because this is the single case where verb choice is linked unambiguously to the position of the speaker alone, it lends further support to the proposition that children learn the rules of speaker anchoring of the deictic verbs before they learn the rules of addressee anchoring.

# 7 *Conclusions*

To arrive at a clearer overview of the material reported in the previous chapters, it is valuable to examine acquisition orders from several perspectives. First, what is the order of acquisition of categories of deictic terms within the population sampled? Second, is this sequence reproduced in individual subjects? Third, within categories, is there an order of acquisition that can be attributed to any single principle? Several such principles are recapitulated, and finally a new one is proposed, whose basic elements are idealized 'language-context' units.

## The sequence of acquisition of classes of deictic terms

Although all of the classes of terms that were investigated in the experiments reported in chapters 2–6 were deictic terms, they were not learned within a narrow span of time. The course of acquisition is spread out at least over the nearly three years represented by the ages of the subjects, and evidence points to an even longer spread. All of the subjects performed at ceiling level on the pronoun task (chapter 4). The youngest one to carry it out was 2;11. Presumably, children who are even younger might also have been successful. Informal experience suggests to me that many children have mastered the person system by the age of 2. Even if they make errors of case assignment, using, for example, *me* instead of *I*, they still adhere to the distinction between first person, second person, and third person. At the other extreme, even the oldest children were not consistently correct on the *come/go, bring/take* task. And that task probed only a portion of the complete semantic structure of these verbs. Clark & Garnica's (1974) study showed that not even all 9 year old subjects were completely successful. Unless the task in this experiment imposed difficulties beyond those of ordinary language comprehension, the span of time for acquiring the deictic signs in English would seem to stretch to at least eight years, matching what is generally considered the period of language acquisition as a whole.

The fact that children have already mastered the personal pronouns means that they have learned something about the organization of meaning that characterizes deictic terms, their inextricable linkage to context. The delay in learning the other deictic terms cannot be attributed to their deictic properties as such. Instead, it must be due to their differing from the personal pronouns in a number of semantic and pragmatic properties. Many of these differences have been discussed in the preceding chapters, but it might be useful to summarize them here.

The order of acquisition of the deictic terms for the sample of children as a group was as follows:

1. Personal pronouns: *I/you/he*
2. *In back of/in front of* (deictic)
3. Demonstratives and locatives: *this/that, here/there*
4. Deictic verbs of motion: *come/go, bring/take*

The relative simplicity of the personal pronouns may reside in any one or perhaps in all of the following factors. The boundaries between the personal pronouns are all clearly defined and absolute. Speakers can only refer to themselves as *I* and never as *you*. They can only refer to their addressee as *you*, never as *I*. By contrast, the boundaries between *this* and *that* and between *here* and *there* are indefinite. The conditions for appropriate use of one of these terms as opposed to another, as for the appropriate use of *come* vs. *go*, are not mutually exclusive. There are many situations in which either one of these opposed terms is suitable.

*In back of* and *in front of* appear to be intermediate in this respect. They are truly polar in that if an adult speaker were to describe any particular situation as 'A in back of B' he would not accept 'B in back of A' as an equally appropriate description (except in the special case when A and B are back-to-back). And the discovery of the polarity of *in back of* and *in front of* in their deictic sense is probably facilitated by the more evident polarity between the nouns *back* and *front* and between nondeictic *in back of* and *in front of*. But there are factors that might also obscure for the child the polarity of the deictic directions. There is evidence that some adult speakers, and perhaps many adults in some contexts, reverse the mapping of deictic *in front of* and *in back of* such that they construe an object on the opposite side of the reference object from themselves as being in front of the reference object.

A second factor obscuring the polarity of *in back of* and *in front of* is that the point of orientation for *in front of* and *in back of* may be either the speaker, or the hearer, or even someone else. In contrast, the point of orientation for the personal pronouns is unique: the speaker, and the speaker alone. The point of orientation for the *this/that* and *here/there* contrasts is also the speaker, but not exclusively so. The addressee may also be included. *Here* and *there* do not *necessarily* contrast the locations of speaker and addressee as *I* and *you* do their identities. The deictic verbs, like *in front of* and *in back of*, admit a broad range of possible points of orientation: the location of the speaker or the addressee or both. Just as a disjunctive concept is more complex than a unitary one the semantic structure of deictic terms with multiple points of orientation is more complex than that of terms with a unique point of orientation.

*This, that, here* and *there* are the only deictic terms whose indexical function is routinely supported by physical gestures of indication. *I* and *you* may also be accompanied by pointing, but *I*, at least, never depends on pointing for disambiguation. On the one hand, the pointing may facilitate children's decoding of the general meaning of these terms as indicators of entities and locations. But, on the other hand, it means that crucial information is being provided in a second medium, perhaps to the detriment of the children's attention to the information available in the linguistic medium. In any case the necessity of pointing is symptomatic of the indefiniteness of the meanings of *this, that, here* and *there*. It suggests that these terms are 'more deictic' than the other deictic terms. The mixture of functions characterizing all of the deictic terms is here particularly heavy in the indexical component, and particularly light in the symbolic one.[1]

---

[1] In the sign language used by the deaf, iconicity and indexicality are exploited more than they are in spoken language. Many referential signs and signs for concrete actions are partly iconic. And some of the indexical symbols of spoken language are purified into indices proper: *I* and *you*, for example, are indicated simply by pointing. Signs for actions can incorporate indexical components, as for example *help*, which means *help me* if the movement is made toward the speaker, and *help you* if made toward the listener (Schlesinger, in press). The principle that is realized in spoken English only in *come* and *go* and *bring* and *take* is apparently productive in sign language.

If human signers can use *direction* of motion to communicate deictic variables, the chimpanzee, Washoe, has done one better. She has in at least one case adapted the *site* of movement for the same purpose. The sign for *tickle* is a movement of the fingers on the back of the hand. When requesting a tickle, Washoe would do this on the back of her addressee's hand.

Although to a lesser extent than in sign language, there is evidence that the deictic terms in spoken language are also quasi-iconic. Across unrelated languages, terms for *here* and *there* exhibit sound symbolism in the form of a consistent contrast between

The categories of deictic terms also differ in the degree to which their polarity is central to their complete meaning. The speaker–hearer contrast between *I* and *you* is coextensive with their meaning. Similarly the spatial contrast between *in front of* and *in back of* exhausts their meaning. But the proximal–distal contrast between *this* and *that* is subsidiary to their general meaning as indicators of 'entities.' With *here* and *there*, it is subsidiary to their general meaning as indicators of locations. And the directional contrast between *come* and *go* is subsidiary to their general meaning as verbs of motion. One can imagine the existence of deictic particles whose entire meaning would be 'in the direction of the speaker' or 'not in the direction of the speaker.' These would have a semantic structure similar to that of *I* and *you* in that the contrast between the terms would be central to and would exhaust their meanings, leaving no residue.

The sets of deictic terms all involve oppositions that can be construed as polar. And the tests of comprehension reported here all probe children's knowledge of these polarities. But the polarities are radically different in the clarity of boundaries between the poles and in the centrality of the polarity to the meanings of the terms. These differences may explain some of the delay between acquisition of one set of deictic contrasts and another.

## Order of acquisition of deictic contrasts by individual subjects

Does the clear gradient of complexity that emerges for the group of subjects as a whole mean that individual children master the sets of deictic contrasts in an invariant order? Must children perform correctly on the easiest task before they can perform correctly on the next harder one, and on both of these before the subsequent one, and on all three before the deictic verbs? Table 19 indicates each subject's success on each of the tasks. In general it can be seen that there is some correlation between performance on various tasks, but this correlation seems to reflect mainly the fact that older children do better than younger ones.

The fact that all the children but one were successful on the personal pronoun task does suggest that perhaps children must learn this system first. But there was one subject (no. 11) who failed to reach criterion on

high front vowels, and vowels that are lower and/or further back (Tanz, 1971). This pattern may also extend to time deixis and person deixis.

TABLE 19. *Performance^a on each experimental test by individual subject*

| Subject | Age | I/you/he | in back of/ in front of (deictic) | this/that | here/there | come/go | bring/take |
|---|---|---|---|---|---|---|---|
| 2 | 2;7 | | − | | | | |
| 3 | 2;7 | | − | | | | |
| 4 | 2;9 | | | + | − | | |
| 5 | 2;10 | | | − | − | | |
| 6 | 2;11 | + | (+) | − | − | − | − |
| 7 | 3;1 | | − | − | − | − | − |
| 8 | 3;1 | | | | | | |
| 9 | 3;1 | + | (+) | | | | |
| 10 | 3;2 | + | − | − | + | | |
| 11 | 3;3 | − | − | − | + | | |
| 12 | 3;3 | + | − | − | − | | |
| 13 | 3;4 | + | − | − | − | | |
| 14 | 3;5 | | | + | − | | |
| 15 | 3;6 | + | − | + | + | − | − |
| 16 | 3;7 | | | − | − | | |
| 17 | 3;8 | | − | + | − | − | − |
| 18 | 3;8 | | − | − | − | − | − |
| 19 | 3;8 | | | | − | | |
| 20 | 3;10 | + | (+) | − | + | − | − |
| 21 | 3;10 | | − | − | − | − | − |

| | | | | | | |
|---|---|---|---|---|---|---|
| 22 | 3;11 | + | + | - | - | - |
| 23 | 4;1 | + | + | + | + | + |
| 24 | 4;1 | + | + | - | - | - |
| 25 | 4;3 | | + | + | - | + |
| 26 | 4;3 | + | + | + | - | |
| 27 | 4;3 | + | + | + | + | - |
| 28 | 4;4 | + | - | - | + | + |
| 29 | 4;5 | + | - | + | - | - |
| 30 | 4;6 | | + | - | + | - |
| 31 | 4;7 | + | + | - | - | - |
| 32 | 4;8 | + | + | - | - | + |
| 33 | 4;9 | | - | + | - | - |
| 34 | 4;9 | + | + | + | + | - |
| 35 | 5;0 | + | - | + | + | - |
| 36 | 5;1 | + | + | + | - | - |
| 37 | 5;1 | + | + | + | - | - |
| 38 | 5;1 | | + | + | + | - |
| 39 | 5;1 | | + | + | + | - |
| 40 | 5;3 | + | + | - | + | + |
| 41 | 5;3 | + | + | + | - | - |

*a* *I/you/he*, +: 14/17 correct; *in back of/in front of*, non-deictic, +: ≥25/27 correct, -: ≤20/27 correct; deictic, +: 8/9 correct, (+): 6/9 correct (6/6 correct on *in front of/in back of*; 3/3 incorrect on *at the side of*); *this/that*, +: 4/4 correct; *here/there*, +: 4/4 correct; *close/far*, +: 4/4 correct; *come/go*, +: 6/8 correct; *bring/take*, +: 6/8 correct.

this task, and yet was successful on another ostensibly more complex one, *here/there*. His failure to reach criterion is itself somewhat questionable since he did not complete the task. Only five responses were recorded for him, but of these five, two were errors. Assuming that he did fail the pronoun task, it is still questionable whether this pattern of failure on *I/you/he* combined with success on *here/there* is a reliable pattern or an accident. Since there were no other subjects who failed on the former, it is impossible to determine the answer to this question.

It would be somewhat surprising if this exceptional pattern were reliable since all other deictic systems logically rest upon the analysis of roles in the speech act which translate directly, without other semantic frills, into the personal pronoun system. This is the only relation of logical dependency that holds between the various sets of deictic terms. All of them depend on the concept of speaker, or on the concepts of speaker and hearer. This is not to say that logic requires that children will learn the personal pronouns before they can learn other deictic systems, only that they must have arrived at the *concept* of speaker and perhaps hearer. It was argued in chapter 3, with respect to *in front of* and *in back of*, that order of conceptual development does not necessarily predict order of linguistic development. Knowledge of the relevant concepts appears to be a necessary condition of correct language use, but may not be a sufficient condition for it. But in this particular case, if we tentatively set aside subject no. 11, the underlying conceptual dependency that holds between deictic terms in general and the roles of speaker and hearer does seem to be directly reflected in the order of language development.

There do not appear to be strict conditional relations among the other three categories of deictic terms. If children perform well on one, they do not necessarily perform well on an ostensibly 'easier' one. There were a number of subjects who were successful on *this/that* or *here/there*, but not on deictic *in front of/in back of* (nos. 10, 11, 15, 16, 23, 29, 35). And some of the very few children who were correct on *come/go* or *bring/take* failed to reach criterion on some of the other deictic contrasts.

The preceding analysis can only be considered tentative because task demands in the several experiments were not identical. However, it is extremely difficult, if not impossible, to construct a single task capable of testing all of the contrasts. Possibly the current deictic verb task discussed in chapter 7 could be adapted in a suitable way by asking children to identify which of several dolls is saying, for example: 'The dog is here in the living room' (*here*/*there*) or 'You shouldn't be upstairs' (personal pronoun).

## Yang and Yin

Osgood (personal communication) has suggested that the principle governing order of acquisition within related sets of terms may be identical with the principle of 'Yang and Yin' whose operation he has described in adult language processing (Boucher & Osgood, 1969; Osgood & Richards, 1973; Osgood & Hoosain, in preparation). A brief statement of this principle is as follows:

basic to human cognitive processes ... is the BIPOLAR ORGANIZATION of cognitions ... [and] the attribution of POSITIVE POLARITY to one of the poles of each dimension of qualification (STRONG and ACTIVE, as well as GOOD, are somehow psychologically positive as compared with their opposites). (Osgood & Richards, 1973: 381)

After providing experimental evidence for the validity of these organizational principles it is proposed that the universality of affective polarity implies that 'UNMARKED (positive) FORMS MUST BE PRIOR IN TIME TO MARKED (negative) FORMS – certainly in the language and probably in the parole of individual speakers' (p. 410).

Some of the implications for language processing of affective polarity have been investigated by French (1974), others by Osgood & Hoosain (in preparation). French showed that it takes less time for subjects to solve three-term series problems (e.g. 'If Bill is taller than Sam and Carl is taller than Bill, who is tallest?') when the comparatives used are relatively positive in affective value (e.g. *taller*) than when they are relatively negative (e.g. *shorter*). French compares the predictions of the Yang–Yin hypothesis with those that H. Clark derives on the basis of the marked–unmarked contrast within the same sets of terms. Usually unmarked terms are affectively positive and the two theories make identical predictions. However, in some contexts they are not. An example from French's study is the word *short* which is marked and usually affectively negative as compared with *long*. In the context of *skirts* however, *short* is (or was) relatively positive in affect as measured with a form of the semantic differential. In three-term series problems involving *long*/*short skirts*, and similar materials where the affective polarity principle and the marking principle make conflicting predictions, French demonstrates that marking predictions either fail to be borne out, or, in some cases, are reversed, supporting the affective polarity principle.

While Osgood does not offer a detailed model of the acquisition of antonymic word pairs by children, he predicts that the operation of the Yang–Yin principle will be manifested here too in the prior acquisition of positive terms. He lists several criteria for assigning positive and negative polarity:

1. an intuitive criterion – 'the feeling that Good is positive with respect to Bad . . .'
2. linguistic (i.e. morphological) marking
3. frequency of usage
4. the use of one term to represent the entire bipolar dimension
5. 'congruence with clearly contrastive forms like *some* vs. *any*' (Osgood & Richards, 1973: 386).

The second and fourth criteria are identical to those which are used in marking theory to identify the unmarked term. Usually all of these criteria converge to select one term. In the cases where they diverge, Osgood places greatest credence in affective polarity as measured by the semantic differential technique.

Let us now examine the predictions made by the principle of Yang and Yin for order of acquisition of terms within the sets discussed in the previous experiments. (Presumably the principle makes no predictions *across* sets of terms.) Table 20 lists Evaluation, Potency, and Activity scores for the terms under investigation. The table is drawn from a compilation by Heise of three published lists of scores. Unfortunately only a small proportion of these sets of terms appear in full on the lists: *close/far, come/go, bring/take*. The words *front* and *back* also appear, but only in their capacity as nouns. Their affective polarity scores, however, are probably related to those that would be found for the spatial relations *in front of* and *in back of*. Single members of other sets also turn up: of the personal pronouns, only *I*, and of the deictic locatives, only *here*. The demonstratives are not listed at all.

In a sense these gaps are as they should be, and could not readily be remedied by carrying out semantic differential tests on the missing words. By definition the deictic terms are problematic for a semantic differential analysis. Unlike symbolic terms, they cannot represent their objects without being in existential relation to them. To a degree,

TABLE 20. *Evaluation, Potency, and Activity scores for selected sets of terms*

| | | E | P | A | | E | P | A | | E | P | A |
|---|---|---|---|---|---|---|---|---|---|---|---|---|
| Personal pronouns | *I* | 1.4 | 0.7 | 1.6 | *you* | — | | | *he* | — | | |
| Demonstratives | *this* | — | | | *that* | — | | | | | | |
| Locatives | *here* | 1.0 | 0.2 | 0.3 | *there* | — | | | | | | |
| Proximity | *close* | 0.4 | 0.7 | 0.1 | *far* | 0.8 | 0.5 | 0.0 | | | | |
| Spatial orientation | *front* (noun) | 0.6 | 0.7 | 0.3 | *back* (noun) | 0.0 | -0.3 | 0.1 | *side* (noun) | 0.6 | 0.4 | 0.4 |
| | | | | | *back.* (adv) | 1.4 | 0.5 | 0.4 | | | | |
| Deictic verbs | *come* | 1.1 | 0.4 | 0.4 | *go* | 1.1 | 0.5 | 0.9 | | | | |
| | *bring* | 1.4 | 0.1 | 0.4 | *take away* | -0.07 | 0.5 | 0.4 | | | | |

TABLE 21. *Predictions for order of acquisition within*

| | I | you | he | front | back | side | this |
|---|---|---|---|---|---|---|---|
| Yang–Yin (Osgood) (Criterion: proximity to Ego) | 1 | 2 | 3 | 1 | 3 | 2 | 1 |
| (Criterion: value on E) | | | | 1.5 | 3 | 1.5 | |
| (Criterion: value on E, P, A (sum)) | | | | 1 | 3 | 2 | |
| Marking (H. Clark) | | | | | | | 2 |
| Positive–negative (E. Clark, H. Clark) | | | | 1 | 2 | 3 | |
| Experimental results (Tanz) | no difference (ceiling) | | | 2 | 1 | 3 | 1 |

ᵃ These predictions were not actually made by H. Clark (E. Clark in fact made the precede marked terms.

although not absolutely, *this*, *that*, *you*, etc. are deficient in meaning when they stand alone, without context, as they do in the semantic differential test. *I* and *here* are the only deictic terms which can still be considered to be sufficiently anchored even in the semantic differential format.

Nevertheless, in lieu of direct measurement, Osgood (personal communication) suggests that one may identify the positive terms on the basis that, in general, proximity to Ego is positive, and remoteness from Ego is negative. He cites, for example, an early study by Solarz, in which subjects were required either to draw a lever toward themselves when they were presented with evaluatively positive words and away from themselves when presented with evaluatively negative words or to do the reverse. Solarz found that it was easier, as judged by response latency, for subjects to pull positive words toward themselves and push negative words away (see Osgood, Suci & Tannenbaum, 1957: 160–1). Accordingly, *I*, *this*, *here*, *come*, and *bring* are positive; *you/he*, *that*, *there*, *go*, and *take* are relatively less positive.

Cooper & Ross (1975), working from a different direction, arrive at similar conclusions. They begin by looking at 'freezes' in natural language, expressions in which the order of conjoined elements is rigidly fixed, for example *here and there* and *this and that*, neither of which is acceptable if reversed to *there and here* or *that and this*. They *sets of deictic terms according to three systematic theories*

| that | here | there | close | far | come | go | bring | take | Correct predic-tions | Wrong predic-tions |
|---|---|---|---|---|---|---|---|---|---|---|
| 2 | 1 | 2 | no pre-diction | | 1 | 2 | 1 | 2 | 2 | 3 |
| | | | 2 | 1 | 1.5 | 1.5 | 1 | 2 | 0 | 3 |
| | | | 2 | 1 | 2 | 1 | 1 | 2 | 1 | 3 |
| 1 | 2 | 1 | 2 | 1 | 2 | 1[a] | 2 | 1[a] | 2 | 3 |
| | | | | | 1 | 2 | 1 | 2 | 0 | 3 |
| 2 | 1 | 2 | 1 | 2 | 2 | 1 | 2 | 1 | | |

opposite predictions), but they are entailed by the proposition that unmarked terms

discover a number of semantic and phonological principles governing order in freezes. The semantic principles include proximate before distant (of which *here and there* is an example), and positive before negative (*for better or worse*). In general, conjuncts referring to properties of the prototypical speaker, or Ego, precede. Cooper & Ross dub this tendency the 'Me First' principle. In sum, what is close, what is good, what is me all take the privileged first position.

For the sets of terms whose affective values on the semantic differential are available, the Yang and Yin hypothesis makes the following predictions: *in front of* and *at the side of* will be learned before *in back of*, *bring* before *take (away)*, and *far* before *close*.[1]

---

[1] The adjective *close* was used in the expression instead of the approximately synonymous *near* for the sake of structural parallelism with *far*. *Close* like *far* requires a prepositional adjunct, while *near* does not.
(1) He parked the car *close to* the house.
(2) He parked the car *far (away) from* the house.
(3) He parked the car *near* the house.
Although *close* and *near* are close to being synonymous, their E, P, and A scores are quite different, sufficiently so that the Yang–Yin hypothesis applied to both of them will predict in one case that the proximal term is learned before the distal term, and in the other case, the reverse.

| | E | P | A |
|---|---|---|---|
| *close* | 0.4 | 0.7 | 0.1 |
| *far* | 0.8 | 0.5 | 0.0 |
| *near* | 1.0 | 0.0 | 0.0 |

On the basis of E scores alone, the Yang–Yin hypothesis predicts that *near* will be

The higher evaluative score of *far* may appear inconsistent with Osgood's generalization that proximity to Ego is positive, but in this case (in contrast with the cases to follow) consistency might be restored by arguing that *far* does not specify remoteness from Ego but rather remoteness in general.

The predictions for the pairs *come/go* are altogether problematic. Taking into account only values on the evaluative features, *come* and *go*, with identical scores, should be learned simultaneously. But we could differentiate the polarities of *come* and *go* by taking into account scores on all three affective dimensions, E, P, and A. Then, overall, *go* has the more positive polarity, and hence should be learned earlier. To complicate matters further, the principle that proximity to Ego is positive predicts that *come* will be learned before *go*. Thus, in trying to apply the Yang and Yin principle to *come* and *go* we can arrive at every prediction that is logically possible: *come* before *go*, *go* before *come*, and neither one before the other. The first three rows in table 21 give predictions for order of acquisition on the basis of the three criteria for identifying the Yang and Yin poles. The last row gives actual results. For the complete set of data reported in this series of experiments, each criterion, consistently applied, yields more false predictions than true ones.

The marking hypothesis

Table 21 also summarizes the predictions made by H. Clark's marking hypothesis which proposes that unmarked terms will be acquired before marked ones. Although the applicability of the hypothesis to *this/that* and *here/there* was questioned in chapter 5, Clark's analysis of *that* and *there* as unmarked terms is represented in the table. Once again incorrect predictions outnumber correct ones with respect to the data from these experiments. The two predictions that were correct (*go* before *come*, and *take* before *bring*) were not actually made by H. Clark but are independently derived from the marking hypothesis. As it happens, E. Clark made the opposite predictions, not specifically on the grounds of the marking hypothesis but on other grounds.

No all-inclusive alternative hypothesis has been proposed in the

---

learned earlier than *far* but *far* will be learned earlier than *close*. On the basis of sums of E, P, and A scores, it predicts that *far* will be learned first, then *close*, then *near*. Both predictions appear to be wrong. Children performed better on *close* than on *far*.

course of this research. It appears that the process of semantic development is neither so invariant across individuals nor so fully determined by any one principle as was believed or hoped when these hypotheses were formulated. The discussion of *in back of* and *in front of* further suggests that the total range of contributing factors will have to be expanded to include, in addition to the complexity of underlying concepts and the complexity of semantic structures, pragmatic factors arising out of language use.

Polarity

Each of the hypotheses represented in table 21 invokes the concept of polarity, the opposition between something 'positive' and something 'negative.' The concept is a broad one. Many different types of conceptual relationships can be assimilated to it: for example, *male/female*, *tall/short*, *over/under*. Lyons (1968) proposes a partial typology of opposites that distinguishes between 'complementarity,' 'converseness' and what he calls true 'antonymy.'

He characterizes complementaries as lexical pairs such that the assertion of one implies the denial of the other *and* the inverse. *Rin Tin Tin is female* implies that *Rin Tin Tin is not male*. And *Rin Tin Tin is not male* implies *Rin Tin Tin is female*. The two categories are mutually exclusive and exhaust the set of all possibilities.

Lyons reserves the term 'antonym' for words such as *big* and *small*. Antonyms are involved, explicitly or implicitly, in making comparisons. As with complementaries, the assertion of one implies the denial of the other. *Jimmy is thin* implies *Jimmy is not fat*. But in distinction from the complementaries, the denial of one member of an antonym pair does not imply the assertion of the other. *Jimmy is not fat* does not imply *Jimmy is thin*. This is because, as Lyons emphasizes, antonyms do not refer to independent qualities, but are devices for grading with respect to some norm on a single quality.

Lyons uses *buy* and *sell*, *husband* and *wife* as examples of the third type of oppositeness, 'converseness.' Prepositional pairs such as *over/under*, *before/after* presumably belong in this category too. Lyons points out certain parallels between the relations of converseness and antonymy. In both cases, the substitution of a term for its converse or antonym is associated with the permutation of other elements in the sentence. *Steve is ahead of Willie* implies and is implied by *Willie is behind Steve* just as *Lew is taller than Julius* implies and is implied by *Julius is shorter than Lew*. Although Lyons does not explicitly formulate the distinction between converses and antonyms, it appears to rest on the notion of gradability discussed above.

Not all opposites fit readily into these categories. Fillmore (personal communication) points out that *in front of* and *in back of*, in their nondeictic sense, do not. While they may appear so at first glance, they are not strict converses of each other. If two trucks are parked back to back, each one is in back of the other. As Lyons himself acknowledges, a more elaborate analysis would yield finer distinctions in categories of oppositeness.

In addition to the numerous standard or 'frozen' opposites in the lexicon, which reflect 'a general human tendency to "polarize" experience and judgment' (Lyons, 1968: 469) the principle of oppositeness can be applied in novel ways. As the poet Richard Wilbur (1973) has noted,

> There's more than one way to be right
> About the opposite of *white*,
> And those who merely answer *black*
> Are very, very single-track.
> They make one want to scream, 'I beg
> Your pardon, but within an egg
> (A fact known to the simplest folk)
> The opposite of white is yolk.'

The focus in psycholinguistic literature on one member of a pair of opposites as positive and the other as negative tends to obscure the variety of conceptual relations involved. And because the outcome of their application is the uniform designation of something as positive and something else as negative in a generally plausible way, it is easy to assume that the criteria for positive and for negative are similar, or at least compatible, when in fact they are not. To take two examples, Bierwisch identifies positive and negative adjectives on the basis of conditions for their appropriate use in sentences. 'A sentence is the less normal the more conditions outside of it have to be met for it to be acceptable' (Bierwisch, 1967: 8). The polar term whose use imposes more conditions on the acceptability of the sentence is designated as the negative term. The ready acceptability of sentence (4) and the dubious acceptability of sentence (5) establish *small* as negative and *big* as positive.

(4) The bed is twice as big as the blanket.

(5) ?The blanket is twice as small as the bed.

E. Clark (1974: 560) also formulates her criteria for positive and negative (verbs) on the basis of 'conditions that have to be met for their use.' The paraphrase suggests a criterion similar to that of Bierwisch. But Clark goes on to identify one term as positive because the conditions that have to be met for its use 'are all positive in form.' A term is negative if the conditions on its use are stated in negative terms. Thus *come* is positive because it requires that 'the speaker or the addressee is at the goal at the time of the utterance or at the time referred to in the utterance.' *Go* is negative because it requires that the speaker is *not* at the goal at those times.

Upon inspection, superficially similar criteria for negative and positive turn out to rely in one case on the *number* of conditions on the use of terms and in the other on the *form* of the conditions. Applied to *come* and *go* the two sets of criteria make different selections of the positive term. The conditions for the use of *come* are stated in positive form, but there are several of them (disjunctive rather than conjunctive). The condition on *go* is stated in negative terms, but it is singular.

In most developmental studies based on an analysis of the polarity of terms, the findings are that positive terms are learned before negative ones. Independent findings that positive is learned before negative can be combined to suggest that children operate according to a very general principle. The uniform outcome tends to obscure the fact that 'positive' and 'negative' may be defined on the basis of different criteria, incompatible criteria, and even mutually contradictory criteria.

The two sets of criteria discussed above are drawn from a universe of discourse that already limits the range of possibilities to a certain degree. Both ostensibly relate to linguistic forms. Formulations on the basis of cognitive polarity and affective polarity which also identify terms as either 'positive' or 'negative,' add to the confusion. It would perhaps be better temporarily to sacrifice the abstract inclusiveness of 'positive' and 'negative' and to use theoretical terms that clearly retain the imprint of the theory they are derived from: 'good' vs. 'bad' (Osgood); 'perceptible' vs. 'nonperceptible' (H. Clark); 'positive conditions on use' vs. 'negative conditions on use' (E. Clark); 'few conditions on use' vs. 'many conditions on use' (Bierwisch), or some more elegant variants of the same. If all of these criteria were discovered to be related or generally convergent in their predictions (an outcome that appears unlikely in the light of the preceding chapters), then the abstract, inclusive rubric of 'positive' and 'negative' would be appropriate and would no longer be misleading.

The perspective that polarity is imposed on the real world and on language in the process of creating semantic structures opens the substantive question of how children learn to apply it. An example from one child (Tanz, 1977) suggests that like other syntactic and semantic fromulae, polarity too can be overgeneralized. At the age of 3, this boy, sitting on the edge of his bathtub, would say when the water was too cold, 'Make it cooler.' When it was too warm, he would request, 'Make it warmer.' In all likelihood he had learned the general structure of bipolar adjectival dimensions in English: augmentation in the direction of one pole is equivalent to diminution with respect to the other pole. Thus on the dimension *good/bad*, if something is 'better' or 'more good,' then it is 'less bad.' Conversely if it is 'worse' or 'more bad,' then it is 'less good.' The dimension of temperature works the same way. If something is 'colder' it is 'not as hot'; if 'hotter,' it is 'not as cold.' Having mastered this system, the child then seems to have applied it to *cool/cold* and *warm/hot* making each of these into a bipolar dimension. Accordingly, 'Make it less cold' becomes 'Make it cooler' and 'Make it less hot' becomes 'Make it warmer.' The overgeneralization constitutes evidence that the child has formulated an abstract concept of polarity.

## Complexity in adult language processing and order in child language acquisition

Osgood, like H. Clark, formulated his predictions for the order of acquisition of terms by children on the basis of gradients of processing difficulty in adults. The assumption is that terms that require more processing time for adults will be acquired later by children. This assumption is not as simple or straightforward as may at first appear. It encounters an apparently insurmountable problem in Osgood's and French's criticism of Clark's model of adult language processing. Clark proposed that certain words are inherently more complex than their antonyms (the marked terms of marked–unmarked pairs). Osgood suggested and French demonstrated that a word which usually requires more processing time than its opposite will in some contexts require less. According to them the vehicle of this contextual effect is affective polarity. The crucial point for this argument is just that there *are* contextual effects which can reverse the relative complexity of two terms.

A model of language processing can accommodate such facts if it is constructed so as to identify the locus of complexity as being somewhere not restricted to the word itself. On the other hand, a model of language acquisition, based on data about the order in which terms are learned, rather than on processing time, cannot by definition accommodate such variation. The very concept of order no longer applies if the order can be inverted. If children perform better on *come* than on *go* in one experiment, and better on *go* than on *come* in another experiment, one can only conclude that at least one and possibly both of the experiments are measuring something other than order of acquisition.

### A note on disagreement between experiments

Three of the four experiments reported here were compared with experiments on identical topics done by other researchers. The record of comparability is dismal. In no case were the patterns of results identical. My experiments were designed and carried out before the publication of the others and hence were neither replications or systematic competitive tests. The differences in procedure were 'accidental' so to speak, rather than constrained by specific theoretical or methodological considerations. I have attempted, chapter by chapter in this book, to suggest possible explanations for the differences in results. In two cases this was done with some degree of confidence and the conviction that one set of results (mine) was right and the others wrong. In one case the selection seemed equivocal. The most serious question that is left open by this set of circumstances is not whether in fact *go* is learned before *come*, but whether results in many other experiments in the literature on semantic development would be overturned if somebody else came along and asked a similar question but conducted the experiment in a way that seemed only trivially different.

## Deixis and egocentrism: language and thought

Deictic terms are curiously pivotal with respect to the issue of egocentrism. Children's use of deictic terms without sufficient linguistic or extralinguistic anchoring is one of the clearest symptoms of cognitive egocentrism to be visible in ordinary interaction as opposed to deliberate experiments. On the other hand, children's comprehension of deictic contrasts clearly reveals the rudiments of decentering. De Villiers & de Villiers have also advanced this claim as follows. They state that as *this/that*, *here/there*, and *my/your* are produced according to the speaker's perspective, 'so comprehension requires a nonegocentric viewpoint' (de Villiers & de Villiers, 1974: 438). In fact the claim may be broadened. Production of these terms, as well as comprehension, requires a nonegocentric viewpoint. Although the child must produce *I/you*, *my/your*, etc. with himself at deictic center, he cannot have grasped this egocentric formula without having understood at some level that other speakers organize the system with themselves at center. Thus, any child who has mastered the shifter properties of *I* and *you* or *me* and *you* in ordinary conversation has achieved some degree of decentering. By the age of 3 almost all children seem to have mastered this system, and it is possible that they have done so considerably earlier. In an experimental task (Flavell et al., 1968) with closely analogous requirements but outside the sphere of language, children of this age were not uniformly successful. Children between the ages of 3 and 6 were seated opposite the experimenter. The experimenter had a set of picture cards and offered to show the children his favorite one placing it so that the picture would be right side up for the children (upside down for the experimenter). He then asked the children to choose their favorite picture and show it to him. If the children failed to place it right side up for the experimenter, they received several prompts, culminating in 'It doesn't look right side up to me; can you show it to me so it does?' (p. 162). The shifting of picture positions between the experimenter's viewing position and the children's viewing position seems analogous to the shifting of *I* and *you* between participants in conversation. Yet a majority of 3 year olds, 4 year olds, and 5 year olds made errors on this task, and some of the 6 year olds did too.

If children can perform certain nonegocentric operations in language before they can perform formally comparable ones outside the sphere of language, it suggests a hypothesis: that the decentering implicit in the correct use of deictic terms not only precedes but helps to prepare for subsequent decentering. The shifting of the deictic center in speech, with its concomitant pattern of shifting *I*s and *you*s, provides children as spectators of speech with an overt scenario of role-switching. And these linguistic details are embedded in a broader pattern of reciprocity, the turn-taking of conversational interaction itself. One participant in conversation speaks, the other listens. Then the roles are reversed. In other types of cooperative interactions, which permit both participants to act simultaneously, underlying patterns of reciprocity may be masked. Thus both in its microstructure (the alternation of deictic terms) and in its macrostructure (the alternation of turns in conversation) language offers demonstrations of and exercises in decentering and role-switching.

In addition to this array of *formal* means by which language may contribute to children's emergence from egocentrism, it provides yet other means. In the *content* of linguistic communication, language offers partial access to other people's inner states. People say 'I want . . .,' 'I like . . .,' and countless other things that indicate their figurative perspectives on situations. It is perhaps because this fact is so obvious that it has gone generally unremarked in discussions of the contribution of language to thinking. But in the oversight, models of cognitive development tend to give the impression, ironically, that children manage to transcend egocentrism by predominantly solipsistic means. This orientation is reflected, for example, in Flavell et al.'s hypothesis that 'the recognition of perspective differences . . . [is] less probable when the perspective in question consists of cognitions, motives, feelings, affects, and the like rather than percepts, especially visual percepts' (1968: 181). The advantage of perceptual perspectives is presumably that children can directly experience their multiplicity simply by changing their physical location. Recognition of the multiplicity of figurative perspectives depends more on inference from observations and can therefore be expected to be more elusive to children, except – and this is the neglected factor – that people talk so much about their 'feelings, affects, and the like,' perhaps more than about their percepts. So information available through language partially compensates for the impossibility of directly experiencing the other point of view.

Language may be of assistance in the discovery of variation in physical perspectives too. When a child, true to his egocentrism, calls from one room to another, 'It's broken!' the parent who is addressed in this manner is likely to say something along the lines of '*What's* broken? I can't see it.'

In the surprisingly partisan debate over the direction of influence between language and thought, the supporters of language might be able to argue that language contributes to the development of thinking in general through its contributions to the process of decentering.

## Deixis: language and context

The deictic terms appeared as a recalcitrant class of terms to linguists because their meanings could not be specified without introducing the extra-linguistic context. But contextual determination of meaning does not seem inherently problematic for children. Numerous studies done from quite different perspectives indicate that for young children, meaning is more profoundly embedded in context than it is for adults. Carter (1975) describes the initial association in one child of the deictic term *here* with a behavioral context of exchange. Only gradually is the term freed from what she calls 'pragmatic reference' to the 'semantic reference' of ordinary locative use. Shatz (1975) has demonstrated that certain contextual factors rigidly determine children's interpretation of the illocutionary force of ambiguous speech acts. If the relevant object is present, she finds that young children invariably interpret questions of the type, 'Can you talk on the telephone?' as requests for action, not information. E. Clark (1972b) has shown that children's interpretation of prepositions at first depends on the properties of the object of the preposition.

This orientation toward the contextual determination of meaning is adaptive. How can pre-linguistic children come to understand language at all if they don't constantly try to interpret it in relation to context? Part of their problem in learning to talk lies in having progressively to *de*contextualize meaning.

In adult language use (production and comprehension), meaning emerges out of the integration of language and context. In child language acquisition meanings are *discovered* through the interpretation of integrations between language and contexts.

A perspective suggested by the studies reported here is that some language-context 'units' are more easily interpretable, more transparent than others. The meanings of terms that relate to contexts in more transparent ways will be discovered earlier. It is not merely the independent complexity of concepts that will govern the sequence of acquisition of words, but aspects of the *relation* between the concepts and the words that attach to them.

In her detailed study of the onset of speech in one child, Jacob, Menn (1978) has also pinpointed such contexts. Jacob's active vocabulary showed a strong bias toward action words, for example *down*, *tap-tap*, and *round*. If he was spinning a top, he was much more likely to say *round* than *top*. As Menn observes, these action words are almost always presented along with the action. Conversely, the actions are usually carried out with the accompaniment of the words. 'The action-words under consideration do not concern the routine activities of getting dressed, eating, being bathed. They are highly focused and are only continued by the adult so long as they seem capable of amusing the child; they are ends in themselves' (p. 65). Such contexts presumably maximize the child's opportunities to discover the meanings of the words. A particularly dramatic example is the context in which Jacob initially used the word *down* – when knocking over tall towers of blocks. Later the word was extended to falling in general and to other uses.

Menn herself sees the facilitating effect of these game contexts in a slightly different way. She suggests that they make it particularly easy for a child to learn, not the name of a concept, but *when* to use the name. Jacob showed passive knowledge of object names considerably before they came into productive use. Menn concluded therefore that he had acquired the referential meanings of the object names, but might have lacked knowledge of when to use them. According to this interpretation, the advantage of the action words which led to their proliferation in early speech was the clear initial contextual delineation of when they should be used. In advancing this interpretation, Menn makes the provocative suggestion that there may be a 'process of learning *when* to talk' worthy of separate study. This suggestion has merit, but will not be discussed further here. The point being stressed here is that properties of language–situation relations bear investigating. Contexts which facilitate learning when to use words may also facilitate initial decoding of the words.

This principle of *language–context transparency* can unify some apparently contradictory findings about acquisition order. The principle emerges out of the concern with language–context links engendered by analysis of deictic terms. But the specific findings, recapitulated here from earlier chapters, have more to do with the acquisition of non-deictic terms.

Previous research has shown that children learn the word *long* before the word *short*, *big* before *little*, etc. One explanation that has been proposed for this pattern is that unmarked terms are learned before marked. An alternative way of capturing the pattern might state that terms indicating the extended end of a dimension are learned before terms indicating the nonextended end. However, the investigation reported in chapter 5 of terms contrasting on the dimension of proximity–distance, challenges the generality of these explanatory proposals. In the case of *this/that*, *here/there*, and *close/far*, there was a tendency for the proximal terms to be learned first. These happen to be the marked terms in each pair, and the terms which apply to the nonextended end of the distance dimension. Is there a single principle that can encompass these apparently contradictory findings? One candidate is the principle of fitness or transparency of the language–context relation.

All objects have length. However, length is a conspicuous property of relatively long objects, an inconspicuous property of relatively short ones. In situations where the adjective *long* is used with respect to a referent, length will be salient. In situations where *short* is used, length will be comparatively less salient. Therefore, it should be easier for a child to discover what people are talking about when they use the word *long* (both in the sense that it has to do with the dimension of length and in the sense that it has to do with extendedness along this dimension), than when they use the word *short*. Brewer & Stone (1975) report that in fact children do learn that *short* applies to the dimension of length only after learning that *long* does so. They claim that children learn the negative polarity of *short* before they learn which dimension it applies to.

All objects also have some relation in space. This relation is conspicuous when objects are close to each other, relatively less so when they are far away from each other: therefore, as above, children should have more ease in discovering what is meant by terms which apply in situations when something is close to something (e.g. *close*) than by terms which apply when two things are far apart (e.g. *far*).

The syntactic property of unmarkedness correlates with the semantic property of extendedness on a dimension. But ease of acquisition seems not to correlate with either the syntactic or the semantic property alone. Rather the crucial factor seems to be the nature of the relation between the language and the contexts it describes. Words that connect with more salient aspects of context are initially easier to decode. This suggests a concept of 'good form' in language–context relations. The criteria of good form can be elaborated further. There can be various kinds of fitness between language and context. All may contribute to ease of acquisition.

A more complex version of good form emerged in the discussion of spatial *in front of/in back of*, and temporal *before/after*. The experiment reported in chapter 3 showed that children comprehend *in back of* better than *in front of*. Previous research had shown that children understand *before* before *after*. Again, the findings are apparently contradictory. And, again, examination of the linkage between each expression and the situation it describes, between language and context, offers a possible reconciliation.

The expression 'X is in back of Y' applies to a situation where the point of reference, Y, is in front, the naturally more salient position. The expression 'Y is in front of X' applies to a situation where the point of reference is in a less salient position. Conspicuousness is a virtue for points of reference. Language that relates to a situation where the point of reference is relatively more conspicuous is presumably easier to decode initially than language relating to situations where it is less so. So again, it should be easier for a child to discover what people mean when they say *in back of* than when they say *in front of*.

In the case of *before* and *after*, it is *before* which occurs in situations where the language–context articulation is most transparent. The convergence of two factors accounts for the transparency differential. A sentence in which two temporal events are conjoined in the order in which they occur has a better 'fit' with reality than one which reverses the order. Sentences with *after* as well as with *before* can be structured to be iconic. But the two sets are iconic in a different form. Sentences with *before* are iconic when the main clause precedes the subordinate clause and when the conjunction occurs between the two clauses. Sentences with *after* can only be iconic when the subordinate clause comes first, and the conjunction occurs 'outside' (in front of) the two clauses. A child will have maximal opportunity to unravel the meaning of a temporal conjunction when iconicity, optimal clause order, and possibly also optimal conjunction position coincide. Therefore it is *before* that is mastered first.

A variety of factors, then, may contribute to the transparency of the language–context relation. Saliency of the relevant details of context in situations where a word is used contributes in one way. An iconic relation between language and context contributes in another way. Both make it easier for the child to discover the mapping between the language fragment and the segment of reality it represents.

Nelson (1974: 276) has proposed a framework for the interaction of the acquisition of conceptual knowledge and word meaning in early development. She suggests a basic sequence of four processes:

1. 'identification of an individual whole'
2. 'assigning individuals on the basis of their functional relations to a synthesized cognitive "chunk" or concept . . .'
3. 'identification of new concept instances by noting the salient stable ("invariant") characteristics of members'
4. 'attaching a name to the concept so formed.'

It is at this fourth step that the idea of 'good form' in language–context or language–concept units becomes relevant. It is not only the nature of the concept or the complexity of the concept that will determine when the child correctly attaches a name to it, but how the name articulates with the concept or the situations in which it is invoked.

Nelson observes that children's earliest words usually refer to things that move or things that children interact with. She implies that the reason for the priority of these words is that the concepts themselves are fundamental. This is plausible, but another explanation that may merit consideration, in line with the principle elaborated above, is that the relation between objects that move and their names is more easily discoverable than the relation between motionless objects and their names.

The latter hypothesis predicts that there will be certain concepts available to children at any age for which they do not have a name. Nelson in fact acknowledges this possibility: 'While it can be stated that naming is dependent upon the existence of concepts, the existence of concepts need not lead directly and easily to naming them.' However, the factors that she mentions which may intervene between the child's forming a concept and attaching a name to it are circumstantial factors; for example the child may form a concept which is not coded by the adult language, or the parents may fail 'to name in appropriate ways' those concepts which they do share with the child. The claim being advanced here is that there are certain stable and systematic variations in word–concept relations which make it easier in some cases and harder in others to discover that the word attaches to the concept.

# Appendix A

*Test items for* in front of/in back of/at the side of. *Fronted object task (chapters 2 and 3)*

Name:                                   *Front/back*      #

Age:

| | | | | | |
|---|---|---|---|---|---|
| 1. Put the ring in back of the boy. | | | 15. Put the ring beside the pig. | | |
| 2. | back ⌣ | cow | 16. | side ∪ | truck |
| 3. | front ⌢ | boy | 17. | back ∪ | chair |
| 4. | side ⌣ | chair | 18. | side ⌣ | house |
| 5. | side ⌣ | boy | 19. | side ⌢ | cow |
| 6. | side ⌣ | girl | 20. | front ⌢ | pig |
| 7. | front ⌢ | truck | 21. | back ∪ | horse |
| 8. | front ∪ | lady | 22. | side ⌣ | horse |
| 9. | back ∪ | house | 23. | back ⌣ | lady |
| 10. | front ⌢ | girl | 24. | back ∪ | girl |
| 11. | front ⌢ | chair | 25. | front ⌢ | horse |
| 12. | front ⌣ | cow | 26. | side ∪ | lady |
| 13. | back ⌢ | truck | 27. | front ⌢ | house |
| 14. | back ∪ | pig | | | |

Subject: ∪

# Appendix B

---

*Items for pronoun alternation test (pilot study–chapter* 4)

*I/you/he* questions

| | |
|---|---|
| *you – I* | 1. Ask X where you should sit. |
| *I – she* | 2. Ask X where I should sit. |
| *he – you* | 3. Ask X where he lives. |
| *I – she* | 4. Ask X if I could sing. |
| *you – I* | 5. Ask X if you can go play. |
| *he – you* | 6. Ask X if he is tired. |
| *his – your* | 7. Ask X what his favorite color is. |
| *my – her* | 8. Ask X what my favorite color is. |
| *your – my* | 9. Ask X what your favorite color is. |
| *he – you* | |
| *me – her* | 10. Ask X if he is scared of me. |
| *he – you* | |
| *me – her* | 11. Ask X if he was given a book by me. |
| *he – you* | 12. Ask X what he doesn't like to eat. |

# Appendix C

*Items for pronoun alternation test (main study–chapter 4)*

*I/you/he* questions

1. Ask X what his favorite color is.
2. Ask X if I have blue eyes.
3. Ask X to guess what your favorite color is.
4. Ask X where he lives.
5. Ask X where my bicycle is.
6. Ask X if you have been good.
7. Ask X where — lives.
8. Ask X if you can visit him.
9. Ask X to guess what your middle name is.
10. Ask X what —'s favorite color is.
11. Ask X what I found yesterday.
12. Ask X if he is scared of me.
13. Ask X where you should put this.
14. Ask X to guess what my favorite color is.
15. Ask X if he is tired.
16. Ask X if —'s eyes are blue.
17. Ask X if I should give you a prize.

# Appendix D

*Test items for demonstratives and deictic locatives (chapter 5)*

Name
Address                                                          *This/that*, etc.

*far*   1. That plate has a penny under it, but this one doesn't.
*near*  2. The plate over here has a penny under it, but the one over there doesn't.
*near*  3. The plate close to the cup has a penny under it, but the one far away from the cup doesn't.
*near*  4. This plate has a penny under it, but that one doesn't.
*far*   5. The plate over there has a penny under it, but the one over here doesn't.
*far*   6. The plate far away from the spoon has a penny under it, but the one close to the spoon doesn't.
*far*   7. That chicken is mine, and this one is Peter's.
           Show me Susan's chicken.
           Show me Peter's chicken.
*near*  8. The pig over here is mine, and the pig over there is Peter's.
*near*  9. The car close to the house is mine, and the car far away from the house is Peter's.
*near* 10. This penny is mine, and that one is Peter's.
*far*  11. The spoon over there is mine, and the one over here is Peter's.
*far*  12. The plate far away from the cup is mine, and the one close to the cup is Peter's.
*near* 13. This plate has a penny under it.
*near* 14. The plate over here has a penny under it.
*far*  15. The plate far away from the spoon has a penny under it.
*far*  16. The plate over there has a penny under it.
*far*  17. That plate has a penny under it.
*near* 18. The plate close to the cup has a penny under it.

# Appendix E

*Test items for deictic verbs of motion* (*chapter* 6)

Name:

Age:

1. Come upstairs and take a bath.
2. Bring a key outside.
3. Take a penny downstairs.
4. Go inside and turn off the light.
5. Bring a seashell upstairs.
6. Take a chicken outside.
7. Go downstairs and close the windows.
8. Come inside and eat lunch.
9. Take a button upstairs.
10. Go outside and play.
11. Come downstairs and watch TV.
12. Bring a pine cone inside.
13. Go upstairs and take a nap.
14. Come outside and play.
15. Bring a rubber band downstairs.
16. Take the chalk inside.

# Bibliography

Amidon, A. & Carey, P. 1972. Why 5-year-olds cannot understand before and after. *Journal of Verbal Learning and Verbal Behavior* **11,** 417–23.

Bartak, I., Rutter, M. & Cox, A. 1975. A comparative study of infantile autism and specific developmental receptive language disorders: 1. The children. *British Journal of Psychiatry* **126,** 127–45.

Bettelheim, B. 1967. *The empty fortress*. New York: Free Press.

Bierwisch, M. 1967. Some semantic universals of German adjectivals. *Foundations of Language* **3,** 1–36.

Binnick, R. 1968. On the nature of the lexical item. *Papers from the 4th Regional Meeting, Chicago Linguistic Society*, pp. 1–13.

　1971a. Bring and come. *Linguistic Inquiry* **2,** 260–5.

　1971b. Studies in the derivation of predicative structures. *Papers in Linguistics* **3,** nos. 2 & 3.

Bloom, L. 1970. *Language development: form and function in emerging grammar*. Cambridge, Mass.: Massachusetts Institute of Technology.

　1973. *One word at a time*. The Hague: Mouton.

Boucher, J. & Osgood, C. 1969. The Pollyanna hypothesis. *Journal of Verbal Learning and Verbal Behavior* **8,** 1–8.

Bowerman, M. 1974. Learning the structure of causative verbs: a study in the relationship of cognitive, semantic, and syntactic development. *Papers and Reports on Child Language Development* **8,** 142–78. Committee on Linguistics, Stanford University.

　1979. The acquisition of complex sentences. In P. Fletcher & M. Garman (eds.), *Language acquisition: studies in first language development*. Cambridge: Cambridge University Press.

Brewer, B. & Stone, B. 1975. Acquisition of spatial antonym pairs. *Journal of Experimental Psychology* **19,** 299–307.

Brown, R. 1973. *A first language*. Cambridge, Mass.: Harvard University Press.

Burks, A. 1949. Icon, index and symbol. *Philosophy and Phenomenological Research* **9,** 673–89.

Carey, S. 1978. 'Less' may never mean more. In R. N. Campbell & P. Smith (eds.), *Recent advantages in the psychology of language: language development and mother–child interaction*. New York: Plenum Press.

Carter, A. 1975. The transformation of sensorimotor morphemes into words:

a case study of the development of *here* and *there*. Paper presented at the Stanford Child Language Research Forum.

Cassirer, E. 1953. *The philosophy of symbolic forms*, vol. 1: *Language*. New Haven: Yale University Press.

Chomsky, C. 1969. *The acquisition of syntax in children from 5 to 10*. Cambridge, Mass.: MIT Press.

Cicourel, A. 1970. The acquisition of social structure: towards a developmental sociology of language and meaning. In J. Douglas (ed.), *Understanding everyday life*. Chicago: Aldine Press.

Clark, E. 1971. On the acquisition of the meaning of *before* and *after*. *Journal of Verbal Learning and Verbal Behavior* **10**, 266–75.

   1972a. On the child's acquisition of antonyms in two semantic fields. *Journal of Verbal Learning and Verbal Behavior* **11**, 750–8.

   1972b. Some perceptual factors in the acquisition of locative terms by young children. In P. Peranteau, J. Levi & G. Phares (eds.), *Papers from the 8th Regional Meeting, Chicago Linguistic Society*, pp. 431–9.

   1973a. What's in a word? On the child's acquisition of semantics in his first language. In T. E. Moore (ed.), *Cognitive development and the acquisition of language*. New York: Academic Press.

   1973b. Nonlinguistic strategies and the acquisition of word-meanings. *Cognition* **2**, 161–82.

   1974. Normal states and evaluative viewpoints. *Language* **50**, 316–32.

Clark, E. & Garnica, O. 1974. Is he coming or going? On the acquisition of deictic verbs. *Journal of Verbal Learning and Verbal Behavior* **13**, 559–72.

Clark, H. 1970. The primitive nature of children's relational concepts. In J. Hayes (ed.), *Cognition and the development of language*. New York: John Wiley & Sons.

   1973. Space, time, semantics and the child. In T. Moore (ed.), *Cognitive development and the acquisition of language*. New York: Academic Press.

   1974. Semantics and comprehension. In T. Sebeok (ed.), *Current trends in linguistics*, vol. 12. The Hague: Mouton & Co.

Coker, P. 1975. On the acquisition of temporal terms: *before* and *after*. *Papers and Reports on Child Language Development* **10**, 166–177. Committee on Linguistics, Stanford University.

   1978. Syntactic and semantic factors in the acquisition of *before* and *after*. *Journal of Child Language* **5**, 261–78.

Coker, P. & Legum, S. 1974. An empirical test of semantic hypotheses relevant to the language of young children. In *Working Papers on the Kindergarten Program: Quality Assurance*. SWRL for Educational Research and Development, Los Alamitos, Calif.

Cooper, W. & Ross, J. 1975. World order. In R. Grossman et al. (eds.), *Papers from the Parasession on Functionalism*, Chicago: Chicago Linguistic Society.

Cromer, R. 1971. The development of the ability to decenter in time. *British Journal of Psychology* **62**, 333–65.

Dent, J. 1971. A preliminary investigation of spatially contrasting items in the speech of the two-year old child. Unpublished paper, Harvard University, Cambridge, Mass.

De Villiers, P. & de Villiers, J. 1974. On this, that, and the other: nonegocentrism in very young children. *Journal of Experimental Child Psychology* **18**, 438–47.

Donaldson, M. & Wales, R. 1970. On the acquisition of some relational terms. In J. R. Hayes (ed.), *Cognition and the development of language*. New York: John Wiley & Sons.

Feldman, C. 1971. The interaction of sentence characteristics and mode of presentation in recall. *Language and Speech* **14**, 18–25.

Fillmore, C. 1966. Deictic categories in the semantics of *come*. *Foundations of Language* **2**, 219–27.

  1971a. 'May we come in?' Lectures on deixis. Unpublished MS. Summer Program in Linguistics, University of California at Santa Cruz.

  1971b. Space. Unpublished MS. Summer Program in Linguistics, University of California at Santa Cruz.

  1971c. Time. Unpublished MS. Summer Program in Linguistics, University of California at Santa Cruz.

  1971d. Deixis I. Unpublished MS. Summer Program in Linguistics, University of California at Santa Cruz.

  1971e. Coming and going. Unpublished MS. Summer Program in Linguistics, University of California at Santa Cruz.

  1971f. Deixis II. Unpublished MS. Summer Program in Linguistics, University of California at Santa Cruz.

Fischer, J. L. 1964. Words for self and others in some Japanese families. *American Anthropologist* **66**, no. 6, part II, 115–32.

Flavell, J., Botkin, P., Fry, C., Wright, J. & Jarvis, P. 1968. *The development of role-taking and communication skills in children*. New York: John Wiley & Sons.

Fodor, J. 1970. Three reasons for not deriving 'kill' from 'cause to die'. *Linguistic Inquiry* **1**, 429–38.

French, P. 1974. Logical and psycho-logical theories of semantic coding in reasoning. Unpublished PhD dissertation, University of Illinois.

Garvey, C. & Hogan, R. 1973. Social speech and social interaction: egocentrism revisited. *Child Development* **44**, 562–8.

Gordon, D. & Lakoff, G. 1971. Conversational postulates. *Papers from the 7th Regional Meeting, Chicago Linguistic Society*, pp. 63–84.

Grice, H. P. 1967. Logic and conversation. Unpublished MS.

  1971. Utterer's meaning, sentence meaning, and word meaning. In J. Searle (ed.), *The philosophy of language*. Oxford: Oxford University Press.

Harner, L. 1976. Children's understanding of linguistic reference to past and future. *Journal of Psycholinguistic Research* **5**, 65–84.

Harris, L. & Strommen, E. 1972a. The role of front–back features in children's 'front,' 'back,' and 'beside' placements of objects. *Merrill–Palmer Quarterly* **18**, 259–71.

1972b. Cues that specify the 'front' and 'back' of simple geometric forms. *Paper presented at the Meetings of the Psychonomic Society.*

1972c. The child's concept of 'in front': a note on the effects of immediately prior experience. Unpublished MS.

Harris, L., Strommen, E. & Marshall, S. 1972. What is the 'front' of a simple geometric form? *Paper presented at the Meetings of the Psychonomic Society.*

Heise, D. 1971. *Evaluation, potency, and activity scores for 1551 words: a merging of three published lists.* Chapel Hill: University of North Carolina, Department of Sociology.

Hill, C. 1978. Linguistic representation of spatial and temporal orientation. *Proceedings of the Berkeley Linguistic Society* **4**, 524–39.

Huttenlocher, J., Eisenberg, K. & Strauss, S. 1968. Comprehension: relation between perceived acts and logical subject. *Journal of Verbal Learning and Verbal Behavior* **7**, 527–30.

Huxley, R. 1970. The development of the correct use of subject personal pronouns in two children. In G. D'Arcais & W. Levelt (eds.), *Advances in psycholinguistics.* New York: American Elsevier Publishing Co.

Jakobson, R. 1957. Shifters, verbal categories, and the Russian verb. Unpublished MS, Harvard University.

Jespersen, O. 1965. *The philosophy of grammar.* New York: W. W. Norton & Co. 1st ed. 1924.

Jones, L. & Wepman, J. 1966. *A spoken word count.* Chicago: Language Research Associated.

Kanner, L. 1949. Problems of nosology and psychodynamics of early infantile autism. *American Journal of Orthopsychiatry* **19**, 416–26.

Kastovsky, D. 1973. Causatives. *Foundations of Language* **10**, 255–315.

Katz, J. & Postal, P. 1964. *An integrated theory of linguistic descriptions.* Cambridge, Mass.: MIT Press.

Keenan, Edward. 1971. Two kinds of presupposition in natural languages. In C. Fillmore & T. Langendoen (eds.), *Studies in linguistic semantics.* New York: Holt, Rinehart & Winston.

Keenan, Elinor. 1974. Conversational competence in children. *Journal of Child Language* **1**, 163–83.

Keller-Cohen, D. 1973. Deictic reference in children's speech. Paper presented at Linguistic Society of America, Winter.

Kuczaj, S. & Maratsos, M. 1974. *Front, back,* and *side*: stages of acquisition. In *Papers and Reports on Child Language Development* **8**, 111–28. Committee on Linguistics, Stanford University, April.

Kuroda, S. Y. 1968. English relativization and certain related problems. *Language*, **44**, 244–66.

Lakoff, G. 1970a. *Irregularity in syntax.* New York: Holt, Rinehart & Winston. 1970b. Linguistics and natural logic. *Synthese* **22**, 151–271.

Lakoff, R. 1974. Remarks on *this* and *that*. In C. Fillmore, G. Lakoff & R. Lakoff (eds.), *Berkeley studies in syntax and semantics, I.* Berkeley: Department of Linguistics.

178    *Bibliography*

Lyons, J. 1968. *Introduction to theoretical linguistics*. Cambridge: Cambridge University Press.

1975. Deixis as the source of reference. In E. L. Keenan (ed.), *Formal semantics of natural language*. Cambridge: Cambridge University Press.

McCawley, J. 1968. Lexical insertion in a transformational grammar without deep structure. *Papers from the 4th Regional Meeting, Chicago Linguistic Society*, pp. 71–80.

1971. Prelexical syntax. In R. J. O'Brien (ed.), *Monograph series on languages and linguistics*. 22nd Annual Roundtable. Washington, DC: Georgetown University Press.

McNeill, D. 1963. The psychology of *I* and *you*: a case history of a small language system. Paper presented at American Psychological Association Symposium on Child Language, April.

1975. Semiotic extension. In R. Solso (ed.), *Information processing and cognition*. Hillsdale, NJ: Erlbaum.

Maratsos, M. 1973. Nonegocentric communication abilities in preschool children. *Child Development* **44**, 697–700.

Menn, L. 1978. *Pattern, control, and contrast in beginning speech: a case study in the development of word form and function*. Indiana University Linguistics Club.

Mountcastle, V. 1975. The view from within: pathways to the study of perception. *The Johns Hopkins Medical Journal* **136**, 109–31.

Nelson, K. 1974. Concept, word, and sentence: interrelations in acquisition and development. *Psychology Review* **81**, 267–85.

Osgood, C. & Hoosain, R. In preparation. Pollyanna II: It is just simply easier for humans to cognize the affectively positive than the affectively negative. University of Illinois, Urbana.

Osgood, C. & Richards, M. 1973. From Yang and Yin to *and* or *but*. *Language* **49**, 380–412.

Osgood, C., Suci, G. & Tannenbaum, P. 1957. *The measurement of meaning*. Urbana: University of Illinois Press.

Piaget, J. 1926. *The language and thought of the child*. New York: Harcourt, Brace & Co.

1954. *The construction of reality in the child*. New York: Basic Books.

1967a. *The child's conception of space*. London: Routledge & Kegan Paul. 1st ed. 1948.

1967b. *The child's conception of the world*. Totowa, NJ: Littlefield, Adams & Co.

Ricks, D. & Wing, L. 1975. Language, communication and the use of symbols in normal and autistic children. *Journal of Autism and Childhood Schizophrenia* **5**, 191–221.

Rommetveit, R. 1968. *Words, meanings and messages*. Oslo: Academic Press.

Rutter, M., Greenfield, D. & Lockyer, L. 1968. A five to fifteen year follow-up study of infantile psychosis. In S. Chess & A. Thomas (eds.), *Annual progress in child psychiatry and child development*. New York: Brunner/ Mazel.

Rosch, E. 1973. On the internal structure of perceptual and semantic categories. In T. Moore (ed.), *Cognitive development and the acquisition of language*. New York: Academic Press.

Schlesinger, I. M. In press. *Some aspects of sign language*. The Hague: Mouton.

Shatz, M. 1975. How young children respond to language: procedures for answering. Paper presented at the Stanford Child Language Research Forum.

Slobin, D. 1973. Cognitive prerequisites for the development of grammar. In C. Ferguson & D. Slobin (eds.), *Studies of child language development*. New York: Holt, Rinehart & Winston.

Tanz, C. 1971. Sound symbolism in words relating to proximity and distance. *Language and Speech* 14, 266–76.

   1977. Polar exploration: *hot* and *cold, cool* and *cold. Journal of Child Language* 4, 477–8.

Teller, P. 1969. Some discussion and extension of Manfred Bierwisch's work on German adjectivals. *Foundations of Language* 5, 185–217.

Werner, H. & Kaplan, B. 1963. *Symbol formation*. New York: John Wiley & Sons.

Wilbur, R. 1973. *Opposites*. New York: Harcourt, Brace, Jovanovich.

# Index

abnormal language development, 57–60; and normal language development, 60
addressee, *see* speaker
adjectives, *see* spatial adjectives
*ahead*, 34–5
Amidon, A., 44, 47–8
anaphora, 73–4
antonyms, 106, 157. *See also* polarity
articles, 3, 70
*ask*, 68
autism, 57–60

Bartak, I., 57n
*before (after)*, 43–8, 167
*behind*, 34–5
best exemplar, 106–7
Bettelheim, B., 57–60
Bierwisch, M., 33–6, 79, 124, 158–9
Bloom, L., 2–3, 56–7
Botkin, P., 8, 162–3
Boucher, J., 151
Bowerman, M., 47, 103, 137–40
Brewer, W., 94, 103, 166
*bring, see* deictic verbs
Brown, R., 2–3, 40, 49
Burks, A., 1

cardinal directions, 16–17
Carey, P., 44, 47–8
Carey, S., 94
Carter, A., 102, 164
Cassirer, E., 70
causatives, 117, 132–40; overextension of, 137–9
Chomsky, C., 68
Cicourel, A., 50
Clark, E., 10, 31, 40–1, 43–4, 47–8, 81–2, 93, 103, 109, 115, 122–33, 138–43, 144, 156, 159, 164
Clark, H., 10, 31–7, 39–40, 42, 47, 78–9, 81–2, 104–7, 123–4, 151, 156, 159–60
clause order, 44–8, 167
Coker, P., 47–8, 103
*come, see* deictic verbs

communication matrix, 14, 40–2
conjunction position, 46–7, 167
conjunctions, 43–8, 167
context, 1, 9–10, 14, 70, 93, 164–8
conversation, 58, 60, 162–3
conversational roles, 6, 50–1, 55, 58–60, 145–6, 150, 162
Cooper, W., 154–5
Cox, A., 57n
Cromer, R., 124

deictic center, 7, 14, 76, 109, 162
deictic locatives, 2–3, 6, 70–107, 145–6, 154–6; and dimension of proximity-distance, 70–5; marked–unmarked analysis of, 78–81; order of acquisition, 87; procedure for studying comprehension of, 83–4; uses of, 72–3
deictic verbs, 6–7, 108–43, 144–50, 154–6, 159; definition, 108–9; idiomatic uses, 109–11; procedure for studying comprehension of, 111–14
deixis, 1–10 *passim*; age span of acquisition, 144; as complex combination of semiotic functions, 2, 7, 146; and concept of speaker and hearer, 55; in demonstratives and locatives, 70–107 *passim*; discourse, 73–4; distinguished from symbolic reference, 2, 4; and egocentrism, 7, 13–15, 161–4; emotional, 73–4; as framework for interpreting autistic speech phenomena, 57–60; and gestures, 84, 92; in idiomatic usage, 74, 109–11; order of acquisition of categories of terms, 144–51, (semantic differential) 152; in personal pronouns, 49–69 *passim*; in prepositions, 11–30 *passim*; as primitive function, 2; as prototype of contextually based meaning, 9–10, 164; in verbs, 108–43
demonstratives, 2–4, 6, 70–107, 145–6, 154–6; and dimension of proximity-distance, 70–5; marked–unmarked

181

www.ingramcontent.com/pod-product-compliance
Ingram Content Group UK Ltd.
Pitfield, Milton Keynes, MK11 3LW, UK
UKHW010046140625
459647UK00012BB/1652